D0821497

Stanislav Grof heads the Grof Transpersonal Training Program and teaches at the California Institute of Integral Studies. He was formerly Chief of Psychiatric Research at the Maryland Psychiatric Research Center, Assistant Professor of Psychiatry at Johns Hopkins University in Baltimore, MD, and Scholar-in-Residence at the Esalen Institute in Big Sur, California.

He is the editor of *Ancient Wisdom and Modern Science* and *Human Survival and Consciousness Evolution*, and author of *Realms of the Human Unconscious, LSD Psychotherapy, Beyond the Brain, The Adventure of Self-Discovery*, and *The Cosmic Game*.

Ervin Laszlo is considered the foremost exponent of systems philosophy and general evolution theory, and is also noted for his work in futures and management fields. Formerly Professor of Philosophy, Systems Science, and Futures Studies at universities in the US, Europe, and the Far East, Laszlo is the author or co-author of 36 books translated into as many as 16 languages including his recent *The Whispering Pond*, and is the editor of another 30 volumes.

Currently, Ervin Laszlo is Founder and President of The Club of Budapest, Founder and Director of the General Evolution Research Group, Science Director of the International Peace University of Berlin, Administrator of the Interdisciplinary University of Paris, Fellow of the World Academy of Arts and Sciences, Member of the International Academy of Philosophy of Science, Senator of the International Medici Academy, Editor of the quarterly *World Futures: The Journal of General Evolution*, and Series Editor of *General Evolution Studies*, and other book series in Germany and China.

Peter Russell earned a first class honors degree in theoretical physics and experimental psychology, and a master's degree in Computer Science at the University of Cambridge, England. He then traveled to India to study Eastern philosophy and on his return began research into the psychology of meditation. Since then his prime focus has been the exploration and development of human consciousness, integrating Eastern and Western understandings of the mind.

Among the first to introduce self-development to the business world, Peter Russell's corporate programs have been applauded by such companies as Apple, American Express, British Petroleum, and IBM. He is the author of many books, including *The TM Technique, The Brain Book, The Creative Manager, The White Hole in Time*, and *The Global Brain Awakens, Waking Up in Time*, and editor of *The Upanishads*.

The Consciousness Revolution

A TRANSATLANTIC DIALOGUE

Two days with
**Stanislav Grof, Ervin Laszlo,
and Peter Russell**

Edited by Ervin Laszlo
Foreword by Ken Wilber
Afterword by Yehudi Menuhin

ELEMENT

Shaftesbury, Dorset • Boston, Massachusetts
Melbourne, Victoria

© Element Books Limited 1999
Text © Stanislav Grof, Ervin Laszlo, and Peter Russell 1999

First published in the UK in 1999 by
Element Books Limited
Shaftesbury, Dorset SP7 8BP

Published in the USA in 1999 by
Element Books, Inc.
160 North Washington Street
Boston, MA 02114

Published in Australia in 1999 by
Element Books and distributed
by Penguin Australia Limited
487 Maroondah Highway, Ringwood,
Victoria 3134

Stanislav Grof, Ervin Laszlo, and Peter Russell have asserted their right
under the Copyright, Designs and Patents Act, 1988, to be identified as the
authors of this work.

All rights reserved.
No part of this book may be reproduced or utilized
in any form or by any means, electronic or mechanical,
without prior permission in writing from the Publisher.

Cover photograph: Telegraph Colour Library
Cover design by Mark Slader
Design by Roger Lightfoot
Phototypeset by Intype London Ltd.
Printed and bound in the USA by Edwards Brothers

British Library Cataloguing in Publication
data available

Library of Congress Cataloging in Publication
data available

ISBN 1 86204 540 2

Contents

Foreword

The Consciousness Revolution is an extraordinary discussion among three of the very finest minds of our time, spirited in its exchange, compassionate in its embrace, brilliant in its clarion call to awaken our conscience and consciousness.

Stanislav Grof is one of the greatest psychologists of this or any time, and will surely be recognized as such by history. His numerous books are already legendary, from *Realms of the Human Unconscious* to *Beyond the Brain* to *The Cosmic Game*. He commands not just the deep respect, but also the genuine affection, of his many friends and colleagues. He is a true pioneer in the modern exploration of the vast and apparently limitless realms of consciousness, and the maps he has drawn of that extraordinary landscape illumine it with a precision and a passion unmatched in our time.

Peter Russell is a brilliant theoretician who brings an astonishing creativity to every topic he touches. In books such as *The Awakening Earth*, *The Global Brain*, and *The White Hole in Time*, Peter focuses again and again on what might be *the* crucial question for the coming millennium: in what ways do changes in consciousness effect changes in the world at large? If we are to usher in a more graceful tomorrow, what changes can we—can you and I—make in ourselves right now that will be conducive to a more positive future? Or is it too late? What then? Peter tackles these intractable issues not only with a keen intellect, but with a truly compassionate heart, and it shows on every page he writes.

Ervin Laszlo can only be called a genius of systems thinking. In books too numerous to mention—my favorites include *The Systems View of the World*, *Evolution: The Grand Synthesis*,

The Choice, The Whispering Pond, and *Third Millennium*—Ervin Laszlo has, probably more than any person alive, intricately spelled out a staggering but often neglected fact: we live in a hopelessly interconnected universe, with each and every single thing connected in almost miraculous ways to each and every other. His work, spanning four decades, has been a clear and consistent call to recognize the richly interwoven tapestry that constitutes our world, our lives, our hopes and our dreams. By rising to a vision of the whole, he has helped countless individuals escape the narrow limitations and depressing fragments that have haunted the modern world for at least three centuries. And it is Ervin Laszlo who, at the suggestion of Uwe Morawetz of the International Peace University of Berlin, assembled the book you now hold in your hands.

The three men met over several days, reports Ervin, to "reflect on the chances of peace in the world, and ended up talking about crisis, transformation, goals and values, worldviews, understanding ourselves and others, art, science, religion, and spirituality. Above all, we talked about consciousness. The state of our consciousness, we soon discovered, was the key issue underlying almost everything else."

And so the conversation began. In the following pages you can follow that absorbing discussion as it unfolded, topic by topic: the importance of consciousness transformation, yes, but also the importance of many other factors as well, from child rearing practices to economic policies to political institutions. And what does it all finally come down to? Perhaps Peter Russell put it best: "We are each of us pulling together the pieces that allow us to make more sense of our lives, and to lead happier, healthier and more caring lives. Each little bit counts. And sometimes, that new little bit can be the piece that suddenly brings many other pieces together, leading to a breakthrough or spiritual awakening. If we think we have to change others, we are missing the point. It makes us think we are special. It puts us in the position of being in command of trying to control the situation. We are all part of the same groundswell. The most important question we need to ask is, how can I put my own life in greater alignment with that groundswell? How can I do my little one-hundred-thousandth worth to facilitate that shift a bit further?"

Stanislav Grof, Peter Russell, and Ervin Laszlo have, in this book as in their many others, done, in my opinion, several lifetimes' worth of facilitating that extraordinary shift a bit further.

Ken Wilber

Preface

In the summer of 1996 Stan Grof, Pete Russell, and I spent two intense days together, first on the terrace of Stan's house in the woods outside Mill Valley, California, and then on Pete's houseboat down in the harbor at Sausalito. We had before us a tape recorder and a stock of questions we had been looking forward to clearing, as much for ourselves as for each other. We had been asked—by Uwe Morawetz of the International Peace University of Berlin—to reflect on the chances of peace in the world, and ended up talking about crisis, transformation, goals and values, worldviews, understanding ourselves and others, art, science, religion, and spirituality. Above all, we talked about consciousness. The state of our consciousness, we soon discovered, was the key issue underlying almost everything else. Can we change and evolve our consciousness so as to transcend the current crisis-prone world "outside," and the current crises besetting our minds "inside"? Having posed the question in this way, we had to go on to discuss how the outside and the inside are related. This, in turn, raised questions about the nature of mind and world, and what we are beginning to find out about them. Then we came back to the world around us and asked how we could make practical and effective use of what we had begun to call the emerging new map of reality.

My own role in the dialogue was twofold: I was a participant, but as designated moderator I also had to see to it that the discussions stayed on track, focused on issues of pertinence to peace in the world. Originally I intended to pose questions that would catalyze discussion on the indicated topics, but soon discovered that this was not necessary. After launching it, the dialogue went on by itself, catching fire as if by spontaneous combustion.

Rather than getting off track, my principal concern turned out to be that we agreed with each other, if anything, rather too much: a dialogue is supposed to have an interplay of contrasting viewpoints. Fortunately our contrasts came, although they were not horizontal, relating to divergent concepts and viewpoints, but vertical, illuminating the major questions from diverse angles and thereby enabling us to bore deeper toward their roots and foundations.

Subsequently, as editor, my task was to ensure that the transcript of our conversation was legible and digestible for the reader. This was not a difficult task. Each of us had checked his own input on the basis of the verbatim transcript and provided a disk with the approved text. This conveyed the assurance that what the reader is seeing in print is what we had actually meant to say. After assembling the checked materials I merely made sure of adequate continuity and consistency in style and expression, and provided an indication of the main topics we had discussed.

We hope that following the progress of our discussions during those two intense and memorable days in California will bring to the reader some of the sense of excitement and passion that we ourselves have felt—and that, on reflecting on what has been said, the reader will carry forward the reflections and the dialogues and reach new insights of his or her own.

It remains for me to thank Uwe Morawetz and his colleagues of the Peace University of Berlin for bringing the three of us together. All of us are grateful to Christina Grof for the hospitality with which she received us in her and Stan's home. The setting for those two days was nearly perfect, and if the ideas that sprung from them have some value, they are no doubt due also to the wonderful conditions under which we exchanged them.

Ervin Laszlo

World in Transformation

Taking stock: the chances of a transformation

L a s z l o : There is a real question about whether we can go on in today's world as we have been until now without triggering breakdowns and crises and endangering peace. This concern is growing, and is expressed in the currency the word "sustainability" is enjoying these days.

Everybody talks about sustainability, but not necessarily understanding what is at stake. It is something new and unexpected in the history of the human species, to live in a way that we cannot continue to live. It would follow from this that we must change. I am afraid that it is not even a question of *whether* we will change, only how *soon* we will change and how *well*. So instead of discussing the usual things that all the think tanks always discuss, just how many trees we should cut down or not cut down and other strategic questions and implications, we should look squarely at the fundamental issue. I suspect that the first things we should be asking are *where* we are, *what* we are, and *how we look at the world and at ourselves*.

We may be approaching the greatest watershed in history. Up to now the great watersheds first came and were then analyzed. But doing so today is too risky. We should form an idea of what is in store for us, and act consciously to improve our chances. To meet this tremendous challenge we need to shed some light on some of the factors underlying the current, epochal change.

Let me begin with a proposition: if we are to survive and

develop, and perhaps already just not to become extinct, our notion of the universe, of the human being, and of the idea of progress and development, needs to be looked at anew.

RUSSELL: You talk of extinction, but what is it that is being threatened with extinction? I do not think we are going to destroy life on this planet. Life is very robust. It has suffered several major species extinctions in the past, and has bounced back. Indeed, if it were not for the major catastrophe that wiped out the dinosaurs 65 million years ago, and 85 percent of the other species of that time, human beings might never have evolved. It may be that human beings are causing another major species extinction. If so, it will be the first time such an extinction has been initiated by one of the planet's own species, which certainly makes it an unprecedented event, but life will still bounce back. If such a major species extinction were to occur we would of course destroy ourselves, but we are not going to destroy life on this planet.

The worst-case scenario is that we destroy the ozone layer. If we do that, life on land would become impossible. Ultraviolet radiation is as dangerous to insects, flowering plants and micro-organisms as it is to human beings. But life in the sea would survive; it existed for billions of years before the ozone layer formed. And when the ozone layer re-established itself, life might once again colonize the land.

I do not think that is the most likely scenario. Far more probable is that we have a series of major economic and environmental catastrophes that lead to the fall of Western civilization. But that would not be the end of humanity. There would probably be pockets of indigenous peoples who survived, and who might well eventually give birth to future civilizations—hopefully wiser than ours. Even the fall of Western civilization need not mean the end of us. We have seen the fall of the Soviet system, but that did not spell the end of all the people there. It meant a lot changed, and hard times for many. But most of the people are still alive.

That may sound like a pessimistic picture, yet I am still optimistic about human beings, about what we can achieve as individuals in the face of adversity. We may be in for hard times materially, but I also believe we stand on the threshold of great changes in the realm of consciousness.

L A S Z L O : Species extinction—unfortunately, the possibility is always there. When Western civilization suffers a major hiccup, it could bring with it the rest, because we have so many arms, so much destructive capability that, if not all life on Earth, we could well destroy all *higher* forms of life. To regenerate it might take thousands, in the worst-case scenario even millions of years. Obviously life will then continue on this Earth, because— unless there is a cosmic catastrophe—the Earth will be around for billions of years more.

But let us take a concrete case. We now have about 40 days of food surplus capability in the US. And this is the only major food surplus country left. If there is a major harvest failure in the poor countries, there will not be the money to buy food imports. And in any case this surplus would not last very long if there is a massive breakdown in Africa or in Asia.

So what happens then? What happens if the carrying capacity of planet Earth moves down from 6 billion, say, to 5 or 4 billion? What happens when the "extra" people get squeezed below the level of subsistence? Major conflicts may erupt, vast epidemics may spread, massive migrations could unfold. The whole system would be shaken. I do not want to dwell on the doomsday aspect of this, but there is certainly a threat we are facing, a very, very major hiccup. That means that we have to change the Western way of looking at things.

I have come back recently from Asia, where I have seen once again how little chance there is for poor people to change what they are doing. They are just eking out a living. The majority of humankind is living very close to subsistence levels, and this, too, is destroying the life support systems.

On all sides we are threatened with a problem, on all sides we have to adapt—and that means changing the dominant consciousness. This is the root of the problem. We have to start thinking differently, feeling differently, and relating to each other and to nature in different ways. Otherwise, the danger we face is enormous. Now we are all in the same boat. Do you think we have the ability to change? Is there a real chance of a major change in consciousness?

GROF: I have been involved for over 40 years in research on non-ordinary states of consciousness induced by psychedelics and by powerful experiential forms of psychotherapy, as well as those occurring spontaneously. During this time, I have seen many instances of profound transformation of individuals. These changes included a significant reduction of aggression and a general increase of compassion and tolerance. As the capacity to enjoy life was enhanced, one could see a significant diminishing of the insatiable drive to pursue linear goals that seem to exert such a magic spell on individuals in the Western industrial world and our entire society—of the belief that more is better, that unlimited growth and doubling or tripling the gross national product is going to make us all happy. Another significant aspect of this transformation was emergence of spirituality of a universal and nondenominational nature characterized by the awareness of unity underlying all of creation and a deep connection to other people, other species, nature, and the entire cosmos.

I have therefore no doubts that a profound transformation of consciousness is possible in individuals and that it would increase our chances for survival if it would occur on a sufficiently large scale. Naturally, it remains an open question whether a transformation of this kind will occur in a large enough segment of the population in a short enough time to make a difference. The practical question is, whether such a change can be facilitated and by what means, and what would be the problems associated with such a strategy. But in the human personality itself there exist mechanisms that could mediate a profound and desirable transformation.

LASZLO: We are now witnessing changes in people's thinking that augur for the coming of a major consciousness revolution. How do you see this? Is it connected with the fact that we are threatened, or is it an independent, merely coincident, occurrence?

R usse ll: I think it is connected. But I do not think the threat is causing the transformation, so much as they both stem from the same issue—the materialistic consciousness of our culture. This is the root cause of the global crisis; it is not our business ethics, our politics or even our personal lifestyles. These are all symptoms of a deeper underlying problem. Our whole civilization is unsustainable. And the reason that it is unsustainable is that our value system, the consciousness with which we approach the world, is an unsustainable mode of consciousness.

We have been taught to believe that the more things we have, the more we do, the more control over nature we can assert, the happier we will be. It is this that is causing us to be so exploitative, to consume so much, and not to care about other parts of the planet, or even other members of our species. It is this mode of consciousness that is unsustainable.

Today only 10 percent of the human population is classed as affluent—meaning that after buying food, clothing, shelter, and other physical necessities, only this proportion of the population has enough money left over for various luxuries. But these people are consuming more than three-quarters of the planet's resources. It is already becoming clear that this is not sustainable—there is no way such a lifestyle can be sustained in the future for the whole human population, particularly for a growing population.

The good news is that there is a simultaneous and widespread deep questioning of this material culture and the material consciousness that underlies it. Here, in the West, where we have the most luxurious lifestyles, more and more people are beginning to recognize that it does not work; it does not get us what we really want. Our system may be very good at satisfying our physical needs. We can get food from the supermarket. We can travel wherever we want, wear fashionable clothes, live in plush houses. But it does not satisfy our deeper, inner, spiritual needs. Despite all these material opportunities, people feel as depressed, insecure, and unloved as before.

THE FIRST DAY · MORNING

GROF: In a sense it is the very fact of saturation and over-saturation of the basic material needs that has created a crisis of meaning and the emergence of spiritual needs in society. For a long time we were kept in the illusion and false hope that an increase in material goods in and of itself can fundamentally change the quality of our life and bring well-being, satisfaction, and happiness. Now the wealth of the Western industrial countries has increased tremendously, particularly in certain segments of society. Many families live in abundance—a big house, two refrigerators full of food, three or four cars in the garage, the possibility to go for a vacation anywhere in the world. And yet none of this has brought satisfaction; what we see is an increase of emotional disorders, drug abuse and alcoholism, criminality, terrorism, and domestic violence. There is a general loss of meaning, values, and perspective, alienation from nature, and a generally self-destructive trend. It is the awareness of the failure of the mainstream philosophy that represents a turning point in the lives of many people. They start looking for an alternative, and find it in the spiritual quest.

LASZLO: It is almost as if there is something in the collective psyche of humanity that is putting up a warning signal, producing some incentive for change.

RUSSELL: It is also something like what the Buddha experienced in his own life, before he became the Buddha. He was born into a very rich family. He was a prince, who had everything he could need—wonderful food, luxuries of all kinds, jewelry, dancing girls, whatever he wanted. But he realized that having all these riches did not end suffering. He saw in his family and courtiers that there was suffering, and he could see suffering in the town outside. So he made it his mission to find a way to end suffering.

Today we are going through a parallel process. In terms of the facilities we have at our disposal most of us are even wealthier than the Buddha was as a prince. And, like him, we are beginning to realize that this does not end suffering, sometimes it only promotes it. There is a deep, collective questioning of what life is all about. Who are we? Why are we here? What is it that we really want? It is not just one of us, but millions upon millions of people are looking beyond the material culture for deeper meaning, inner peace, and a way to satisfy their spiritual hunger.

L A S Z L O : There are signs of hope. If all people would believe that their happiness is bound up with their current material standard and with improving it along the usual notions of progress—as having more and more of everything—then we would not see any light at the end of the tunnel. If there is a real change in people's way of thinking, there is hope that a more adapted culture is emerging.

G R O F : I have worked with people who had a major goal in life that required decades of intense and sustained effort to achieve. And when they finally succeeded, they became severely depressed, because they expected something that the achievement of that goal could not give them. Joseph Campbell called this situation "getting to the top of the ladder and finding that it stands against the wrong wall."

This obsession with linear pursuits of various kinds is something that is very characteristic for us, individually and also collectively for the entire Western culture—pursuing the *fata Morgana* of happiness that always seems to lie in the future. Things are never satisfactory the way they are—we feel that something has to change. We want to look different, have more money, power, status, or fame, find a different partner. We do not live fully in the present. Our life is always a provisorium, a preparation for a better future. This is an empty, insatiable pattern that keeps driving our life irrespectively of our actual achievements. We see around us examples of people who have already achieved what we think would bring happiness—Aristotle Onassis, Howard Hughes, and many others—and realize it did not work for them, but we do not learn from their example. We keep believing that it would be different in our case.

At the same time, I have repeatedly seen people who were able to discover the psychological roots of this pattern and were able to break it or to reduce its power in their lives. They typically realized that this attitude toward life is closely connected with the fact that we carry in our unconscious the unfinished gestalt of the trauma of biological birth. We were born anatomically, but have not really digested and integrated the fact that we escaped the clutches of the birth canal. The memory is still alive in our unconscious. This imprint then functions as a stencil through which we see the world and our role in it. Like the fetus struggling in the confinement of the birth canal, we cannot enjoy the present situation. We seek a solution in the future—it always seems to be ahead of us.

The existentialists call this strategy autoprojecting— imagining oneself in a better situation in the future and then pursuing this mirage. This is a loser strategy whether we achieve the goal or not, since it never brings what we expect from it. It leads to an inauthentic way of life that is incapable of bringing true satisfaction—a "rat race" or "treadmill" type of existence as some people call it. The only solution is to turn inside and complete this pattern in experiential work, in the process of psychospiritual rebirth. Full satisfaction comes ulti- mately from the experience of the spiritual dimension of existence and of our own divinity, not from the pursuit of material goals of any scope or kind. When people correctly identify the psychospiritual roots of this pattern of insatiable greed, they realize they have to turn inside for answers and undergo inner transformation.

LASZLO: Is this realization on the increase?

GROF: It certainly seems to be. I feel that it has something to do with the fact that more and more people are coming to the conclusion that autoprojecting is a bankrupt strategy that does not work, since they have experienced the failure of material success to bring satisfaction or, conversely, their pursuit of external goals runs into insurmountable problems. In either case they are being thrown back on themselves into their inner world and begin a process of inner transformation. Also the failure of the strategy of unlimited growth on a global scale might be a contributing factor in this process.

Unfortunately, many people who are experiencing a radical transformation of this kind are misdiagnosed as psychotic by psychiatrists and put on suppressive medication. My wife Christina and I believe that there is a substantial subgroup of individuals currently treated for psychosis who are actually in a difficult psychospiritual transformation, or "spiritual emergency," as we call it.

RUSSELL: In a way our whole culture is going through a spiritual emergency. Much of it can be traced back to the changes that went on in the late sixties. For the first time a large section of society began to challenge the current worldview; they saw another way of operating, another way of relating to people and to the world that was not based on the old materialistic paradigm.

In hindsight a lot of what was going on then may appear to us now as naïve, but the key insights have not changed, and they have deeply affected our culture. Back then, meditation was seen as something pretty weird. Now lots of people practice some form of meditation—you even find meditation being taught in corporations. It has become a respectable activity. Similarly with yoga. In the sixties it was avant garde; today it is practiced by millions of people.

Or take therapy. In the past, being in therapy suggested you had major psychological problems; there was something seriously wrong with you. Today in California there is something wrong with you if you are *not* in therapy. Even those we regard as psychologically healthy are seeing that they may still not be living their full potential, and are recognizing that they need help in discovering the attitudes and thought patterns that may be holding them back.

Thirty years ago there was little interest in self-development.

Today it is mainstream. When I was a student at Cambridge in the sixties, the main bookstore, one of the largest in Britain, had just one shelf where you could find books on esoteric and spiritual teachings. Today you can go into any city and find at least one, and probably half a dozen, bookstores devoted to consciousness and metaphysical ideas.

The growth of this interest is reflected in the best-seller lists. For several years now, somewhere around 50 percent, and sometimes more, of the top-selling books have been books on self-development, spirituality, or consciousness. This is what people are reading, this is what they are interested in. You can see similar patterns in movies, television, magazines, even on the Internet. It is a groundswell that is growing rapidly.

LASZLO: This raises a question that has always fascinated me and continues to fascinate me more and more, and that is the possibility that we, as individuals, are not prisoners of our own cranium and locked in our skin, but are intimately tied in with one another, and possibly with all life on this planet. So that when there is a situation like we have at present, where a real danger is facing all of us, there is something which, though most people are not aware of it consciously, is penetrating their mind, putting up warning signs, focusing on change, providing impetus. Perhaps it is not entirely exaggerated to say that there is such a thing as a mind of humanity, something like a noosphere, a collective unconscious operating in and around all of us, which is now beginning to show up in the consciousness of individuals. There may be forces operating in this world beyond the usual economic and political and social forces. This is important for our survival—the situation would look almost hopeless uniquely in light of the usual factors; with them we will never change in time.

The fact is that there are time-lags built into the dynamics of our world, and they are considerable. We would have had to change yesterday, so to speak, to head off the crisis tomorrow. But if there is something in our collective unconscious which can penetrate into our individual consciousness, then the situation is more hopeful.

GROF: I could not agree more. The events in the world do not always follow a logical linear progression. Both you, Ervin, and I are from Eastern Europe and have been following with great interest the political developments there. I think you agree that had somebody told us a week prior to the Berlin wall going down that this was going to happen, we would have laughed and dismissed it as a silly fantasy. It would have seemed equally implausible that, after 40 years of totalitarianism and despotic political control by the Soviet Union, Gorbachev would simply lose interest in the satellite countries, such as Hungary, Czechoslovakia, Poland and the others, and give them freedom. And it certainly would not have been easy to predict that practically overnight, the Soviet Union would simply disintegrate and cease to exist as a superpower. There was no way these events could have been anticipated and foreseen simply by extrapolating the past. There had to be some other factors at work.

LASZLO: That these processes occur in a nonlinear, leapwise fashion, we should have known, knowing the way complex systems operate and transform. Major transformations are unpredictable in detail—all we can anticipate is that they will bring some radical novelty. But is such a revolutionary kind of change also relevant to the processes that hold sway in our mind? Is there also a change in consciousness coming, a change that is strong and pronounced already in the next few years, even though right now we have only the faintest indication of it? Could we be on the threshold of a major revolution in consciousness?

RUSSELL: It is certainly possible. If interest in personal development keeps growing at its current rate, and this interest is translated into a real change of consciousness, then we could see a process of positive feedback leading to an exponential acceleration in inner awakening. The more people wake up, and the more we learn about what fosters inner awakening, the more conducive the social environment becomes for further awakening, encouraging yet more people to awaken, and even faster—which in turn makes it even easier for more people to undergo a change in consciousness. This could well cumulate in a collective leap in consciousness.

Death and rebirth: extinction and renewal

RUSSELL: While a revolution in consciousness is possible, there are many other scenarios as well. As we just said, we are living in unpredictable times. The pace of change is so fast, and the world so complex, that no one can predict what the world will be like in ten years' time, or even five years' time. The only thing that is certain is that we are going to see many unexpected changes. Some of them may be disasters, some of them may be major political turnarounds, and some of them could be major shifts in consciousness. But I do not think we can predict exactly *what* will happen or *how*. We have to be prepared for the totally unexpected, and that could be anything.

LASZLO: Or it could be nothing. That would be worse.

RUSSELL: It will not be nothing.

LASZLO: What I mean is that we may not be here to experience it.

RUSSELL: We may not. And this is certainly a very real fear. It is also a fear that we need to look at more deeply, because it is clearly tied in with the fear of death.

Our personal death is the only thing we are certain of in our lives. Being aware of it is a price we pay for being conscious of our own individuality, and being able to look ahead into the future. Death is the only inevitability; yet most of us live our lives as if it were never going to happen. We avoid thinking about it. We live our life in denial of the one thing that cannot be denied.

The same is true on a collective level. We fear the end of our world, the end of our civilization. But maybe that, too, is inevitable. After all, no civilization in the past has lasted forever. Why should ours be any different? Both therapists and spiritual teachers tell us that accepting and even embracing our own personal mortality is one of the healthiest and most liberating things we can do. Perhaps we should do the same collectively—accept and even embrace the end of the world as we know it.

Usually we do the opposite. We deny it, try to fight it. We do not want it to happen—probably because we do not want to let go of the comfortable lifestyles to which we have become so attached. But we may have to accept it in the end. And that acceptance may be the trigger that opens us to new possibilities, to a much richer, more spiritual way of looking at life.

L ASZLO: Yet I believe that humanity as a species has the capacity to transform and renew itself.

R USSELL: In principle, yes. But I think we also need to open up to the possibility that it is too late, that time has run out.

L ASZLO: That is a feeling I, too, am having increasingly. Indeed, time may be running out.

R USSELL: We should be open to this possibility. The greatest danger may lie in repressing it.

G ROF: Based on the experiences and observations from my work, I tend to see death in a larger context, from a spiritual perspective. In non-ordinary states of consciousness, the psychological encounter with death is the key element in psychospiritual transformation. When death is confronted in a symbolic way in inner self-exploration, it is conducive to a spiritual opening, a mystical experience. Encounter with actual biological death can be used for the same purpose. For example, in the Tantric tradition in Tibet and in India, one has to spend some time in cemeteries and burning grounds and experience contact with dying people and corpses. It is seen as an important part of spiritual practice.

When we confront death internally, what happens is that we do not experience biological demise but what can be called ego death. We discover in the process that we are not the body ego or what Alan Watts called the "skin encapsulated ego." Our new identity becomes much larger—we start identifying with other people, with animals, with nature, with the cosmos as a whole. In other words, we develop a spiritual or transpersonal self. This leads automatically to a greater racial, cultural, political, and religious tolerance and to heightened ecological awareness. And these are changes that could become extremely important in the current global crisis.

Something similar happens also in people who have near-death experiences (NDEs). Typically they are profoundly transformed, with a new set of values and a new life strategy. They see life as being very precious and do not want to lose a single minute of it. They do not want to waste time by autoprojecting. This means they really live in the present, in the here and now.

In retrospect, all the time we spent chasing some mirage of future satisfaction is wasted time. When we can look at our life retrospectively, from the moment of imminent death, only the time when we lived fully in the present appears to be time well spent. This is the great lesson that comes from confrontation with death, whether this is a brush with biological death or a symbolic encounter with it during meditation, in psychedelic sessions, holotropic breathwork, or in spontaneous psycho-spiritual crises.

RUSSELL: I have just been through an experience with a close friend who died just a few weeks ago. I knew she was dying of cancer and had been prepared for it for over a year. When she did pass away, my immediate reaction was, I, too, need to die. I didn't quite understand the feeling at first, but as I let it in, I saw it was about needing to die on the ego level in order that I could live more fully.

A few weeks later I met her boyfriend and found that he had had a very similar experience, though much more profoundly. He said that when she died, he also died. The realization of how inevitable death is and what it means affected him so deeply that he has come alive in a new way. He said: "I'm not going to waste another moment of my life. I'm not going to refuse another opportunity to really live life." In a way, part of him died and part of him came alive through having his beloved die. It was a very powerful and moving experience.

L A S Z L O : I had a profound personal experience recently, when I was in Auroville, India. One day I could not sleep all night, I did not know why. The next morning I got the news that my mother had died. The following day I went up north, to Dharamsala, to see the Dalai Lama. I spent three days there, including what the Tibetans consider the critical day, the fourth day after someone has died. This is the day the spirit of the departed begins its transition. Being with the Tibetan lamas, my experience was that, no, this is not the end. There is a continuity. It was a very profound experience, and it was very different from what it would have been in a Western setting. It has stayed with me in some ways ever since. The loss is there, but the sense is that it is not an absolute loss, not the end of something, but a transformation.

G R O F : This sounds very much like the kind of awareness with which people emerge from powerful transformative experiences: death is not the final and absolute end of existence; it is an important transition into another form of being.

L A S Z L O : In the East knowledge about life, death, and rebirth has been handed down for thousands of years. Now we are rediscovering these insights also in the West.

GROF: Indeed, much of this has been known for centuries or even millennia in different parts of the world. When I started doing psychedelic research some 40 years ago, I came into it equipped with Freudian psychoanalysis, which was a very narrow and superficial model of the psyche. In serial LSD sessions, all people that I worked with sooner or later transcended the Freudian framework, which is limited to postnatal biography and the individual unconscious. They started having a wide range of experiences uncharted by Freudian theory and Western psychiatry. I spent three years patiently mapping these experiences, believing that I was creating a new cartography of the human psyche. As I saw it then, this was made possible by the discovery of LSD, a powerful new research tool. However, when I completed this map to such an extent that it included all the major experiences I was seeing in psychedelic sessions, I realized that the new map was not new at all, but a rediscovery of a very ancient map.

Many experiences included in my cartography were described in the anthropological literature on shamanism, the most ancient healing art and religion of humanity. In shamanism, non-ordinary states of consciousness play an absolutely critical role both in the initiatory crisis, that many novice shamans experience at the beginning of their career, and in the shamanic healing ceremonies. Similar experiences were also known from the "rites of passage," important rituals first described in the book of the Dutch anthropologist Arnold van Gennep.

Rites of passage are conducted in native cultures at the times of critical biological and social transitions, such as the birth of a child, circumcision, puberty, marriage, menopause, aging, and dying. In these rituals, the natives have used similar methods ("technologies of the sacred") for inducing non-ordinary states as the shamans—drumming, rattling, dancing, chanting, social and sensory isolation, fasting, sleep deprivation, physical pain, and psychedelic plants. Typically, the initiates have profound experiences of psychospiritual death and rebirth.

Many experiences in my extended cartography of the psyche can also be found in the literature on the ancient mysteries of death and rebirth which were popular and widespread in the ancient world from the Mediterranean to Mesoamerica. They were all based on mythologies describing the death and rebirth of gods, demigods, and legendary heroes—the stories of Inanna and Tammuz, Isis and Osiris, Dionysus, Attis, Adonis, Quetzalcoatl, and the Mayan Hero Twins. In the mysteries, initiates were exposed to various mind-altering procedures and had powerful death and rebirth experiences.

The most famous of these rites were the Eleusinian mysteries conducted every five years for a period of almost 2,000 years in Eleusis near Athens. A fascinating study by Gordon Wasson (who brought the Mexican magic mushrooms to Europe), Albert Hoffmann (the discoverer of LSD), and Carl Ruck (a Greek scholar) showed that the key to the events in the Eleusinian mysteries was the sacred potion *kykeon*, a psychedelic sacrament made of ergot and similar in its effects to LSD. When my wife Christina and I visited Eleusis, we found out that the number of people who were initiated at Eleusis in the main hall (*telestrion*) every five years exceeded 3,000. This had to have an extraordinary influence on ancient Greek culture and through it on European culture in general. This has not been acknowledged by historians.

The list of the initiates in the Greek mysteries reads like a "Who is Who in Antiquity." It includes the philosophers Plato, Aristotle, and Epictetus, the poet Pindar, the playwrights Euripides and Aeschylus, the military leader Alkibiades, and the Roman statesman Cicero. Considering these facts, it became obvious to me that our discoveries in the research of non-ordinary states of consciousness were actually rediscoveries of ancient knowledge and wisdom. All we did was to reformulate them in modern terms.

R USSELL: Yes, we are rediscovering a wisdom that has been rediscovered many times in many cultures. What we are exploring is the nature of the human mind—and the essential nature of mind has not changed significantly over human history. What has changed is what we are conscious of, our knowledge, our understanding of the world, our beliefs, our values. These may have changed considerably. But the ways in which the mind gets trapped, we get caught by fear, sucked in by our attachments, driven by our desires, have changed very little. The essential dynamics of the mind are the same today as they were 2,500 years ago. That is why we can still derive so much value from reading Plato or the Upanishads.

Throughout human history there have been those who have recognized that there are great untapped potentials of human consciousness. Many of these have discovered for themselves a different mode of awareness, one that leads to a greater sense of inner peace and a richer, more harmonious relationship with the world around, less restricted by fear and self-centered thinking patterns. These are the saints, sages, and shamans that have arisen in every culture. Many of them have tried to help others to awaken to this more liberated mode of consciousness, and have developed a variety of techniques and practices aimed at freeing the mind from its various handicaps. In one way or another they were all seeking to help people step beyond the egoic mode of awareness.

LASZLO: Could the spread of these insights and techniques in the Western world have a major effect on what we are doing? On how we are relating to each other—how we are relating to nature?

GROF: I certainly believe that it could profoundly influence our worldview and change our practical approach to life. If we look at the worldview of Western industrial civilization and compare it with those found in ancient and native cultures we find a profound difference. One aspect of this difference involves the depth and quality of our knowledge of the material world. Western science clearly discovered many things, from the world of astrophysics to the world of the quantum, concepts that the ancient and native cultures did not know anything about. That is quite natural, something that comes with time and progress, it is as one would expect.

However, there is another aspect of this difference that is truly extraordinary and surprising. It is the fundamental disagreement concerning the presence or absence of the spiritual dimension in the universe. For Western science, the universe is essentially a material system that created itself. It can be, at least in principle, fully understood with reference to natural laws. Life, consciousness, and intelligence are seen as more or less accidental side-products of matter. In contrast, ancient and aboriginal cultures have a concept of an ensouled universe that has many ordinarily invisible domains and includes the spiritual dimension as an important aspect of reality.

This difference between the two worldviews has usually been attributed to the superiority of Western science over primitive superstition. Materialistic scientists attribute any notion of spirituality to a lack of knowledge, superstition, wishful fantasies, primitive magical thinking, projection of infantile images to the sky, or gross psychopathology. But when we take a closer look, we see that the reason for this difference lies elsewhere. After 40 years of consciousness research, I feel strongly that the true reason for this difference is the naïveté and ignorance of Western industrial civilization in regard to non-ordinary states of consciousness. All the ancient and native cultures held non-ordinary states of consciousness in high esteem. They spent much time developing safe and effective ways of inducing them and used them for a variety of purposes—as the main vehicle for their ritual and spiritual life, for diagnosing and healing diseases, for cultivating intuition and extrasensory perception, and for artistic inspiration.

R u s s e l l : I mentioned earlier that much of this current growth of interest in consciousness can be traced back to the sixties. It is interesting that much of this change was triggered by non-ordinary states of consciousness. This was the first time in our history that psychedelics had been used on a wide scale, and it led to a large number of people experiencing the states that we

THE FIRST DAY • MORNING

are talking about. And it had a very deep impact. Many of these people came away profoundly changed by that experience. And it did not go away.

I remember Timothy Leary being asked in the early eighties where all the flower children had gone. His response was that they had gone to seed. And that is exactly what happened. Today those people are in their late forties or fifties. A few did drop out, but most dissolved back into society, got married, had kids, and built a career for themselves. Quite a few have now risen to respectable and powerful positions in society. I know some who are presidents of large corporations, some are senior figures in the entertainment business, others hold important positions in education, government and health care. For many of them, the vision and insights they gained in the sixties remain. And some are quietly using their newfound influence to let a little of that vision seep into the world.

Another interesting development in recent years has been the growing scientific interest in consciousness. In the past science left consciousness to one side. And for good reasons. You cannot measure it like you can other things; you cannot pin it down; you cannot even define it easily. The physical world seems to function perfectly well without any need to include consciousness, so there was little pressure to explore the subject. But today things are changing. This is partly the result of our increasing knowledge of brain function, which is bringing the question of consciousness into focus. Scientists and philosophers are beginning to ask: What is consciousness? How does it relate to brain activity? How has it evolved? And where does it come from? In the last few years we have seen a series of international scientific conferences devoted to the issue, and a new scientific journal, *The Journal of Consciousness Studies*.

This opening to the exploration of consciousness is partly the consequence of scientific developments, but I think it also owes a lot to large numbers of people having the experience of non-ordinary states of consciousness. If there is one thing that these experiences do it is to revolutionize one's attitude to consciousness. As you said, Stan, one cannot have a profound experience of this nature and not come away realizing that there is something severely missing from our models of mind and reality.

I think that we are now in the middle of a profound and widespread revolution in our view of reality. The old materialistic models are beginning to lose their grip, and we are gradually piecing together a new understanding. And the direction we are going suggests that the new model will be one that includes mind and consciousness as a fundamental aspect of reality.

LASZLO: This change is coming about in spite of mainstream scientists not knowing it, or even wanting it. Sometimes one is changing or innovating despite of oneself—without knowing where the changes are coming from. In my own case, I had an experience about six or seven years ago that is relevant here. I came across an idea that I thought was just a fleeting notion, yet perhaps interesting to explore. I wrote a small essay on it that was published only in Italian, called *The Psi-Field Hypothesis*. Then I forgot all about it, but other people would not let me forget. For several years after the book came out people kept calling me and referring to it, and doing research on it. Then it occurred to me that maybe there is something more to it. I am not rid of the idea yet . . . on the contrary, it has got hold of me unexpectedly. I am working on it right now, and the more I work on it, the more I find that there is really something in the cosmos that corresponds to a psi-field—to an interconnecting subtle information field.

Such intuitions are not entirely conscious. I am not sure why I got involved with this concept; there was nothing in my mind before that which would have prepared me for it.

I find that this sort of thing is occurring increasingly in today's world. It is almost like one would be driven to carry out some explorations. This may also be a sign of the times, a consequence that we are living in a particularly unstable and transforming era in history. The question is, are these changes fast enough? Will they have a sufficient effect? Of course, they are not entirely predictable. But can we be reasonably hopeful about the effect these changes will have?

A revolution in consciousness?

RUSSELL: Let me tell you about something that happened to me around four years ago, which had a major impact on me and my work. I was traveling around the United States on a lecture tour, promoting my new book, *The White Hole in Time*. The basic theme of my talks was very much along the lines that we have been touching on here. I was suggesting that the global crisis we are facing is, at its root, a crisis of consciousness, and if we are going to save the world then we need to be doing more than just saving the rainforests, curbing pollution, reducing carbon emissions and stopping the destruction of the ozone layer. We also have to free ourselves from the egocentric, materialistic mode of consciousness that is giving rise to these problems. Otherwise we are only tackling the symptoms of the problem, not the root cause; only patching over the deeper problem.

I found myself listening to myself talking and thinking, there is something wrong here. There is a dissonance between what I am saying and what I am actually thinking. I was not saying what I really believed. It was what I had believed in the past, but my views had gradually changed and I realized I no longer felt quite the same way. I was talking out of my past, and that made me uncomfortable.

It came to a head one day in Dallas. I was doing a radio show—one where people phone in with their questions and comments—and I was astounded to realize that most of the callers were denying that there was any environmental crisis at all, or at least not one that affected them or that they had any responsibility for. They firmly believed that the greenhouse effect and the thinning of the ozone layer were a left-wing conspiracy. If there were any environmental problems they were not here in the USA, and there was no way they were going to consider changing their lifestyle. They were not even prepared to listen to anyone who questioned the American way of living.

That made me realize that the only people I was actually having any real communication with were those who were already thinking as I was. I was preaching to the converted. While that does have some value—we all need inspiration, and reminding of the things we know deep within—it was not going to have any significant effect on the vast numbers who currently have no interest in changing their consciousness.

The initial reaction to this experience was one of hopelessness and depression, and it brought to awareness a number of things that I had not been looking at. I thought, supposing that we do manage to get the majority of people interested and motivated in this area, how rapidly can consciousness change? I looked at myself. Here I am, a person who has for some 30 years been practicing meditation, and exploring consciousness in various ways. I have certainly benefited from it, and have changed in various ways; but I'm still a long way from being enlightened. I am still caught in many of my old thinking habits, my ego-mind is still in control for much of the time, and I am still far from being a model citizen. After all these years, I still have a long way to go—and I am somebody who has been deliberately working on his own inner growth. If it is such a slow process, what hope is there for people who aren't even consciously trying to move in that direction? Is there really any hope that humanity can wake up in time?

Then I thought, suppose that by some magic we were all to wake up right now, would that be the end of our problems? Suppose extraterrestrials were to land tonight and miraculously change our consciousness, or a new Buddha were to appear on television and we all "got it" overnight? Even then, if we all woke up and became fully enlightened beings, the crisis would not disappear. The problems we have already set in motion, the environmental devastation, the population explosion, the decimation of the rainforests, the greenhouse effect—these are all going to take a long time to turn around.

As you can imagine, this added to my despondency. Then I remembered some work I had been involved in with the oil company Shell, on future scenarios. Shell has a group of futur-ists dedicated to looking 30 years ahead and mapping out possible scenarios. The goal is not to predict the future—they know that is impossible—but to explore a range of scenarios, and to take these into account in major decisions. If you are thinking of building a new oil refinery in Venezuela, for instance, you are making some very long-term decisions, and want to look at how that decision might pan out under a range of different economic, political, social, and environmental scenarios. You want to make sure you have all your bases covered.

I realized that I had been totally focused on the "we can save the world if we change our consciousness" scenario. I call it scenario A. I had been totally suppressing scenario B—the scenario that says it is already too late, the shit is hitting the fan, and there is nothing we can do about it. It is not a pleasant scenario at all, which, of course, was the principal reason I had not been willing to let it fully into my awareness. But uncomfortable as it is, it was clear that it is also a very possible scenario, and therefore one that should be given full consideration.

So I decided, Okay, let's look at this. What would the world be like under scenario B? Well, there are a lot of possible subscenarios, but what is common to them all is that there is a lot of hardship and suffering. There is psychological pain; things people were used to doing may not be possible anymore, many comforts to which we have been accustomed may no longer be available, life might be very difficult indeed. There may also be physical pain and suffering. Who knows what will happen if the food supplies start dwindling, as, Ervin, you suggested that they might.

So I asked myself, what is going to be needed in those circumstances, what is going to help? It became clear that one area that would become very important would be caring, compassion, and community. I remembered a Yugoslavian friend from Zagreb, who lived through the war there amidst the social chaos and devastation produced by the bombing. I asked her how she managed to come through it, and she said what made it bearable was being able to sit down with friends, have a cup of tea and some caring human contact.

How do we develop caring and compassion? That brought me right back to the core of Buddhism. How do we let go of our attachments, our desires, our fears, and all the other "stuff" that keeps us locked in our own private worlds, concerned only with our own well-being? Then the realization hit me—and this was totally fascinating--I realized that this is essentially the same path I had been arguing for under scenario A. If we were going to heal the planet and save ourselves through a change in consciousness, then we have to free ourselves from our egocentricity, from our attachments to things. Scenario B was pointing in exactly the same direction. To survive these hard times we need to free ourselves from our attachments and self-centeredness, and become more loving, caring beings. Either way the path is the same—the same inner awakening is called for.

Seeing this freed me up. If the work we need to do is the same on either scenario, then which scenario actually occurs is not so crucial. For me it is no longer a case of raising consciousness in order to save the world, or in order to cope with a failing world. Either way raising consciousness is important; either way the same kind of inner work is needed. As a result I found myself free to carry on the same path, but without an attachment to a particular outcome. That was a big shift for me.

LASZLO: On the worst-case scenario we would certainly need a major change in consciousness, much compassion, even to stay alive. Do you think such "consciousness revolution" would come about in the world on its own?

RUSSELL: Achieving true compassion takes a lot of inner work. Sometimes hardship can foster compassion, but not always. It depends how open and ready a person is. So we still need to focus on the inner work, on freeing our minds from fear, from outdated belief systems, from the controlling grip of the ego-mind. We still need to develop greater inner stability, and free ourselves from our material attachments. The more we do that now, the more flexible and compassionate we are likely to be when the need arises.

The turning point for me was the realization that the inner work is the same, and that what is needed is to get on with it in my own life. Changing consciousness is valuable in itself. Maybe it will lead to a world in which we can avoid some of the catastrophes. Maybe it will not. But either way it is absolutely essential.

GROF: People living in ancient and traditional cultures regularly experienced a changed, non-ordinary consciousness in various socially sanctioned rituals. They experienced identification and deep connection with other people, with animals, with nature, and the entire cosmos. They had powerful encounters with archetypal beings and visited various mythological realms. It is only logical that they should have integrated these experiences and observations into their worldview. The worldview of traditional cultures is a synthesis of what people experienced in everyday life through their senses, together with what they encountered in visionary states.

Essentially the same thing is happening to people who have the opportunity to experience non-ordinary states of consciousness in our own culture. I have yet to meet a single person from our culture, no matter what his or her educational background, IQ, and specific training, who had powerful transpersonal experiences and would continue to subscribe to the materialistic monism of Western science. I am the founding president of the International Transpersonal Association (ITA). We have had 15 international conferences with a stellar list of presenters, many of them academicians with impressive credentials. When they had personal experiences of non-ordinary states and studied them in others, they all found the Newtonian/Cartesian worldview seriously lacking. Sooner or later, they all moved to a much larger alternative vision of the cosmos that integrated modern science with perspectives similar to those found in the mystical traditions, Eastern spiritual philosophies, and even native cultures. They embraced a worldview that describes a radically ensouled universe permeated by Absolute Consciousness and Superior Cosmic Intelligence. I believe that something similar would happen to our entire culture if non-ordinary states became generally accessible.

Dimensions of the Transformation

Consciousness-shift in society, paradigm-shift in science

L A S Z L O : Clearly, from what we have said this morning it is evident that we agree that what we need is a fundamental change in consciousness and that there are indications that consciousness *is* already changing fundamentally. When we look at some aspects of this change, should we not ask, what is the major difference between the consciousness that is needed, and the consciousness that is still dominant today?

G R O F : I see two different elements in the current crisis that require radical change in consciousness. The first one has been part of human nature since time immemorial, and the second is a product of the modern era.

Human history has always been dominated by unbridled violence, Erich Fromm's "malignant aggression," and by insatiable greed and acquisitiveness—always wanting more. Throughout the ages, we have seen racial, cultural, political, and religious intolerance exploding in wars and bloody revolutions, invasions, conquests, and domination.

The modern contribution to the problem comes from materialistic science and its profound ideological impact. The dominant scientific worldview in a sense justifies and endorses a life strategy based on individualism and competition rather than synergy and cooperation. In the context of Darwinian and Freudian thinking, it is perfectly natural, legitimate, and understandable to pursue selfish, egotistical goals at the expense of others. It reflects our true nature which is based on primitive instincts and is fully consistent with Darwin's principle of the "survival of the fittest."

There are also significant ecological implications of the old paradigm that Pete talked about, the attitude first formulated by Francis Bacon that leads to a mindless exploitation of nature, the plundering of non-renewable resources, and global pollution. So we need both new strategies that would allow the transformation of destructive human tendencies, such as malignant aggression and insatiable greed, and a profound revision of our value system and scientific worldview. In our culture, where we have enormous, and in some regards even inflated and unrealistic, respect for science, the importance of the paradigm shift should not be underestimated.

LASZLO: Stan, you speak of today's deep respect for science, but also mentioned the dominance of the Cartesian, Baconian and Newtonian view. It seems to me that the respect we have for science is for a completely outdated science.

GROF: Yes, that is the problem.

LASZLO: One of the difficulties in developing a new consciousness and having it spread among people is the break it implies between the emerging worldview suggested by the new sciences, and the worldview that is dominant because it is the view of the scientific and technical establishment. So there seems to be a need also to update our concept of what the sciences are really telling us. Because society at large is years behind the leading edge of science.

GROF: This is exactly what I wanted to say. Science has enormous prestige and what most people mean by science is the Newtonian–Cartesian paradigm dominated by monistic materialism. And this way of thinking has some dire consequences for us individually, as well as collectively. This is why we need a combination of a deep inner transformation with a radical revision of the outdated scientific worldview. This is why I feel, Ervin, that your work is extremely important for our future. Besides offering a brilliant synthesis of the existing general theories, such as the conceptual frameworks of David Bohm, Rupert Sheldrake, and Ilya Prigogine, it also makes it possible to bridge the gap between science and spirituality. In a culture where science enjoys great respect and authority, if its message is distinctly anti-spiritual, it seriously inhibits people's interest in the spiritual quest.

LASZLO: We assume that science is an open enterprise, that it can readily change when new data are coming to light. But many scientists are highly conservative—actually they are just as conservative as their colleagues in the academic world in general. So it is a great challenge asking scientists to assume responsibility for communicating knowledge that is meaningful to people and that at the same time opens up new perspectives. In the conservative tradition of the hard sciences there is nothing meaningful but mathematics and the readings on our instruments. One does not care what it all means, as long as the equations work out and check with the observations and the readings. This has become a dangerously outdated attitude. Fortunately, this conservatism does not plague the creative and innovative edge of science where most of the great breakthroughs occur. There, we see an opening to new ideas, to new worldviews, even to a new spirituality.

GROF: I think it is fascinating to compare the situation in contemporary psychology and psychiatry with what happened at the leading edge of physics in the early decades of this century. How little it took for the physicists to make the radical conceptual transition from Newtonian physics to Einstein's theories of relativity and from there to quantum theory! By comparison, we have an enormous amount of data showing that the current scientific understanding of consciousness and the human mind is inadequate and untenable. This evidence comes from comparative religion, anthropology, experimental psychiatry, experiential psychotherapy, parapsychology, thanatology, and other fields. Yet all this material has been completely ignored by mainstream science.

A very clear example can be drawn from thanatology. We have repeated observations suggesting that people in near-death situations often have the capacity to perceive the environment without the mediation of the senses—they observe the resuscitation procedure of their bodies from the ceiling, witness events in other rooms of the same building, or even travel in a disembodied state to various remote locations. These are the so-called "veridical out-of-body experiences." The general public is well aware of this phenomenon from popular books, talk shows, and even Hollywood movies. In a recent study, Ken Ring has shown that these experiences occur also in people who are congenitally blind. This observation alone should be enough to topple the myth that consciousness is a product of the neurophysiological processes in the brain and lead to a radical revision of the current paradigm. And there are numerous observations similar to this in transpersonal psychology and in modern consciousness research.

RUSSELL: As observations such as these are taken more seriously we are going to see a major paradigm shift taking place in science. It could be the most significant shift ever in Western thinking, and we could already be in its early stages. Thomas Kuhn, who introduced the idea of paradigms some 30 years ago, pointed out that the shift occurs in several stages. First is the discovery of anomalous data that do not fit in with the current model of reality. Because no one is questioning the current model, the anomalies are usually ignored, or even denied. Then, as the evidence for the anomalies begins to accumulate and can no longer be easily ignored, the existing model is modified to try and accommodate the errant data. In the classic case of the Copernican Revolution, the anomalous data was the fact that the planets did not move in smooth circular orbits, as they should if they were moving around the Earth in circular orbits. The medieval astronomers tried to accommodate these peculiarities by adding epicycles to the orbits—these are the curves described by circles rolling around circles. And when these were still not sufficient to explain the observations, they added epicycles to the epicycles—circles rolling around circles rolling around circles—resulting in a very cumbersome model. But the basic worldview was still not questioned.

We are at a similar stage with the phenomena of consciousness. As far as Western science is concerned, consciousness is a great anomaly. There is nothing in the scientific model of reality that predicts that human beings should be conscious, and absolutely no way of accounting for it. Yet consciousness is the one thing of which we can be absolutely certain. This was what Descartes was getting at with his famous *cogito ergo sum*; I can doubt my perceptions, I can doubt my thoughts, I can doubt my feelings, but what I cannot doubt is that I do perceive, think and feel, that I am a conscious being. So scientists today are in the strange situation of being continually confronted with the existence of their own consciousness, and yet having absolutely no way of explaining it.

In the past, science simply ignored consciousness. It did not seem necessary to include it; anyway, they were studying the physical world, not the mind. Today, science is finding that it can no longer simply ignore the subject of consciousness, and it is in the second stage of a paradigm shift, that of trying to stretch the current model so as to somehow incorporate the anomaly. Some scientists are looking to quantum physics, some to information theory, others to neuropsychology. But no one is getting very far in any of these directions. The reason is that they are all trying to explain consciousness from within the existing space–time–matter paradigm. The fact that they are not making any appreciable headway suggests to me that they may all be on the wrong track. What is needed is a completely new model of reality, one that includes consciousness as a fundamental aspect of reality, as fundamental as space, time and matter—perhaps even more fundamental.

This is the third stage in Kuhn's process, the creation of a radically new model that explains the anomalous phenomena. We are not there yet. We see the old paradigm is not working. We see a lot of its cracks and flaws. But few people dare to think beyond the box of the space–time–matter model. Yet that is what it is going to take for a new model to emerge. At the moment, however, science is still firmly stuck in the old model.

LASZLO: We are hanging on to the outdated paradigm, treating it as reality rather than as a model. We—that is, most scientists, and people who look to science as a source of truth—believe that it is literally true.

RUSSELL: Yes. This is what always happens with paradigms. People believe that the model is the truth, and their whole reality is seen from within that model.

GROF: Gregory Bateson wrote and talked about the confusion of map and territory. He said it is like coming to a restaurant and eating the menu instead of the meal.

LASZLO: Luckily sometimes there are subtle changes even in the august world of science that have tremendous and generally unforeseen consequences. Even a map that was taken for reality for 300 years can fall by the wayside. This is what happened in the first decade of this century, when Einstein's relativity was accepted in place of Newton's classical mechanics. But just why did that happen? After all, physicists could always explain the same phenomena in the light of quite different theories. There is always more than one explanation for everything.

GROF: Why indeed was Einstein's interpretation of the results of the measurement of the perihelion of Mercury during the solar eclipse accepted? It was not really an accurate prediction, it just was closer to the actual measurements than one could derive from the Newtonian model.

LASZLO: Actually one could get practically the same predictions out of Newtonian physics if one assumes the ballistic theory of light. Assume that light—the stream of photons—has mass so that the photons are attracted gravitationally to the mass of the Sun and of other celestial bodies. You would get a curved path, the same as if you assumed that space—or space-time—was curved.

GROF: Then why is it that Einstein's theory was accepted, rather than Newton's?

LASZLO: In the final count it appears that this was due to something that is almost an esthetic factor in science: simplicity and elegance. Here the simplicity and elegance of the basic mathematics of a theory is intended. In the special theory of relativity first proposed by Einstein the equations of motion remain invariant even when motion is accelerated. The famous "relativistic invariances" make the equations come out constant and elegant. When encountering the strange effects that came to light at the turn of the century—black-body radiation among others—physicists did not have to add *ad hoc* suppositions and theory-saving devices to maintain the validity of their theory.

Centuries earlier Copernicus accomplished a similar feat with his heliocentric theory. He did away with the epicycles added to the epicycles astronomers needed to conserve the validity of the old geocentric astronomy. Copernicus was convinced that nature loves simplicity. Certainly, scientists love it in their theories, which are sophisticated enough already without making them more complex than is absolutely necessary. This is a major consideration in the acceptance of theories in modern science.

RUSSELL: I have always been fascinated by the simple and invariant aspect of the cosmos. I started my career as a mathematician, drawn to it because of the simplicity and beauty of the subject. What I found most fascinating—it was something of a personal epiphany—was the discovery that there is one basic equation underlying the mechanics of the entire physical world. Everything reduces to one form or another of Euler's equation, or what in layman's terms is called the wave equation. It is a very simple formula, but one with enormous power. It applies to the swing of a pendulum, the dynamics of the atom, the propagation of light, the movement of the planets. It is so simple and so beautiful. If you had asked me then if there is a god, I would have said it was in mathematics.

But what is even more remarkable is that mathematics, which is a creation of the human mind, should bear any relationship to physical reality.

GROF: One would expect that the capacity of mathematics to model phenomena in the material world would be seen as a major argument against the Cartesian split between *res cogitans* and *res extensa*, mind and matter. How could a system that is a product of the psyche correctly predict phenomena in an entirely different realm?

LASZLO: Scientists tend to consider a single set of phenomena and try to explain it with the most simple and beautiful math. But the simplicity and the beauty of the math changes with the range of the phenomena one considers. If you look at both the physical world and the biological world, a different set of basic concepts will apply than if you look at just one or the other of these worlds. If you look also at the world of the human psyche, and take in the more esoteric reaches of experience— for example, the transpersonal and near-death experiences we were talking about earlier—then one's system of explanation will change again. You will be looking for other, still more general explanatory concepts. Perhaps in the near future we will have basic and beautiful math embracing a larger chunk of reality—a chunk that will also include human consciousness together with the living world and the physical universe.

R USSELL: Yes, I think that is the direction we are moving— the new paradigm could emerge soon. All it takes is for someone to pull all the pieces together in a radically new way and produce a theoretical model that is able to account for the world of mind along with the world of matter. I find it very exciting; it has become the focus of much of my own work over the last few years. At the moment we see consciousness as something which emerges from space, time and matter, something that appears as a result of physical activity in the human nervous system. But what we are moving toward is the complete opposite. I believe that, sooner or later, we are going to have to accept that consciousness is absolutely fundamental to the cosmos, not something that arises from matter.

In a way this is not new at all. It is what many of the ancient traditional wisdoms have spoken about. Most of Indian philosophy, for example, is predicated on the assumption that consciousness is absolutely fundamental. Science currently dismisses such ideas, but in the end it may have to accept that there may be something to them after all.

L ASZLO: We are moving toward a new culture of which science could be a part, of which the ancient wisdoms could be a part and in which they could both find a new integration. At its best, this is not just a recovery or a rehearsal of the past, but a new synthesis.

G ROF: Yes, what we are moving toward is not a simple regression and return to the old ideas, but a progression along a spiral, where some of the old elements appear on a higher level as part of a creative synthesis of the ancient wisdom and modern science.

RUSSELL: I like the idea of a spiral; it contains both the idea of returning to where we have been, yet with something more added. I don't think we are going to see a simple return to ancient traditions. They were appropriate for their time, but we live in a different world, in a different social climate, and with a different understanding of the cosmos. What is needed now is contemporary wisdom, appropriate to contemporary times. The core message is the same. It is what Aldous Huxley called the Perennial Philosophy, the same basic wisdom recurring time and again in many different cultures at many different times. But the actual formulation of it varies considerably. What we need today is a formulation in contemporary terms that is comprehensible to ordinary people and relates to life today.

I think this is what the consciousness revolution is all about. We are rediscovering that eternal wisdom for ourselves in contemporary terms, and making it relevant to a world in which science and reason prevail.

A role for spirituality

GROF: Let me return to the challenge we talked about earlier, the synthesis of the mystical and the scientific worldview. There is a general sense in academic circles that science and its materialistic monism have disproved and disqualified once and for all everything that is spiritual and religious, from primitive folk beliefs to the great mystical traditions. I believe that this reflects, besides a fundamental misunderstanding of the nature and function of science, also a confusion between spirituality and religion. I see this as a serious problem and believe that reconciliation between science and spirituality is impossible without a clarification of this issue.

L A S Z L O : Then how would you define spirituality—in what way is it different from religion?

G R O F : Spirituality is a private matter reflecting the relationship between the individual and the cosmos. By comparison, religion is an organized activity that requires a particular place and a system of appointed mediators arranged in a hierarchy. Ideally, a religion should provide for its members, means and support for spiritual experiences. However, often that is not the case! As a matter of fact, personal spiritual experiences are quite threatening for organized religions, because they make their members independent of the organization, of the belief system. Mystics do not need mediation, they have a direct line to the divine, for spirituality is based on direct experiences of a radically different perspective on consensus reality, or of some other dimensions of reality that are ordinarily hidden. These are experiences that occur in non-ordinary states of consciousness. The study of these experiences is the subject of transpersonal psychology. It is a realm of phenomena that should be seriously researched and the results should be included in the comprehensive scientific worldview of the future.

At the cradle of all great religions were visionary states, the transpersonal experiences of their founders—Buddha's experience of enlightenment under the Bodhi tree, Mohammed's miraculous journey, or Moses' vision of Jehovah in the burning bush. The Bible is full of descriptions of such experiences— Ezekiel's vision of the flaming chariot, Jesus' temptation by the devil, Saul's blinding vision of Jesus on the way to Damascus, or St. John's apocalyptic revelation in his cave on the island of Patmos.

However, when religions get organized, believers hear about these experiences in sermons and read about them in sacred scriptures. Direct access to the divine is not available any more and it is often not even acceptable. If a person would have a true mystical experience in one of today's churches, an average priest would probably send him or her to a psychiatrist. Once a religion is organized, direct transpersonal experiences occur mostly only in its mystical branches or in monastic orders where there is actual spiritual practice—meditation, fasting, prayers, and so on.

There is a fundamental difference between religion and mysticism. There are religions without spirituality and there is spirituality without religion. Organized religion needs to convince people that they have to come regularly to a specific place and relate to the system to have the right relation to the divine. For the mystics, nature and their own bodies play the role of the temple. Their connection with the divine is direct and does not need any mediators, particularly not those who themselves did not have the experiences and are nothing but appointed officials. What mystics can benefit from is a supportive community of fellow seekers and teachers who are more advanced on the path than they are.

Authentic spiritual systems are based on centuries of systematic exploration of the psyche using well-defined mind-altering technologies. They are results of a process that in many ways resembles the scientific method.

LASZLO: The philosopher Alfred North Whitehead said something very beautiful: he said that science as well as culture progresses by the coming of a great mind who throws new, more integrated and comprehensive light on a particular domain of experience and inquiry. His ideas are adequate in general, but inconsistent in detail. Then come his followers who reduce it to consistency and in the process lose sight of the original insight. It becomes sterile, mere dogma. The dogma collapses in time in its turn, and then comes a new integrator with another creative insight, and the process starts all over again. This happens in religion as well.

RUSSELL: It is inevitable that this should happen. Religions, as we have just said, have always started from individuals, or sometimes from groups of individuals, who have had a deep personal experience of liberation. In some way or another they have woken up to the truth, and sought to pass that realization on to others. That is how the teachings originally arose.

Unfortunately, the teaching is never received in the same state of consciousness as that in which it is given. The teacher is talking from an enlightened point of view, while the disciple is trying to understand from a less enlightened consciousness, and inevitably something is lost. So long as the teacher is around, he or she can try to correct errors and ensure that the disciple receives the teachings correctly. But once the teacher has died, the teachings are passed on from one person to another. Each time something is lost or not fully understood, or something is added that was not in the original. It is a bit like the game of Chinese whispers in which a message is passed around a circle of people. Each time a slightly different message gets passed on, and by the time it arrives back at its starting point it may be completely different from the original.

The same occurs with spiritual teachings, but on a much grander scale. The message is being passed not just from one person to another, but from one generation to another, from one culture to another, and it is often translated from one language to another. Each time bits are lost and bits are added, and the version that reaches us may bear little resemblance to the original. It is what I sometimes call "truth decay." It is the reason why the major spiritual traditions appear so different. Yet they all began from very similar experiences. We need to rediscover that common core, rather than worry about differences.

This is why it is important not to try to resuscitate previous spiritual traditions. We would inevitably be resuscitating a corrupted version of the original. Our challenge is to get back to the source, the living source based on personal experience, rather than doctrine and dogma, and to live that experience in our own lives.

LASZLO: The mystical traditions were present already in the Greek schools, even in the pre-Socratics, although their insights were not formulated in ordinary language, for public dissemination. What had been so formulated was already a compromise, for consumption by society. The essence of the teachings was something one did not hear or read about, but had to live. It is not surprising that what we get in the tradition handed down to us is just the dry bones, not the living spirit.

GROF: What we need in today's world is more spirituality, not more religions. Organized religions in their present form are part of the problem, not part of the solution. In many parts of the world, religious conflicts are the main source of violence.

RUSSELL: We must remember that organized religion is not a reflection of an enlightened mode of consciousness. Its goals may be laudable, but the people promoting or defending it are generally as unenlightened as the rest of us. Sadly, they are often another reflection of what is wrong with society.

It all comes back to self-centeredness. Self-centeredness at the biological level is okay, we need to be self-centered to make sure we feed ourselves and keep ourselves out of harm's way— we need that basic level of self-centeredness to keep ourselves physically surviving. But we also apply the same self-oriented mode of thinking in areas where it is totally inappropriate. You could say that we have forgotten what our real self-interest is.

In the final analysis what everybody wants is to be at peace. We want to feel okay, to feel in balance within ourselves. Our society says you get that inner experience by what you have, what you do, what you experience in the outer world. This leads to an intrinsic self-centeredness. We are always thinking, what can I take, what can I do, in order to be happy. Where do I stand in other people's eyes, what belief system should I adopt?

This search underlies not only much of our materialism, it is also the reason why we get trapped into religions. I may believe that this belief or this teaching is going to save me; by following this path I am going to be okay. And then we get very attached to our particular faith, and go to all sorts of lengths to defend and protect our chosen path. In this way religion can easily end up very self-centered. Which is ironical, because religion sets out to release people from their self-centeredness.

LASZLO: Religion is also a social phenomenon, a question of collective identity. We need to belong to a community, a social, cultural group, or a religious congregation. This need is filled differently today than it was in the Middle Ages, when the religious congregation was the key community to which one belonged, at least in Europe. Now we have the national and the regional communities, and within them all sorts of levels down to the neighborhood ethnic communities. Belonging to a religious group or congregation provides a sense of identity only to a limited number of people. And belonging to such a congregation has even less to do with gaining access to some ultimate truth. For the most part the doctrines disseminated there just draw boundaries between the "in" group and the rest—between the "believers" and the "heathens."

GROF: Traditionally, what organized religion has done is to unify a group of people by focusing on specific archetypal figures and themes and claiming that they are unique. This typically brought the group into conflict with other groups who had chosen another form of representing the divine and relating to it—Christians against Jews, Hindus against Muslims, Sikhs against Hindus, and so on. Sometimes an organized religion did not even do a good job of uniting its members within its own sphere, under its own umbrella. A prime example of this has been Christianity within which a fierce conflict between Catholics and Protestants has raged since the end of the Middle Ages and has caused much bloodshed and suffering.

By contrast spiritual experiences provide direct access to the sacred dimensions of existence. They reveal the unity underlying the world of seeming separation, the divine nature of creation, and our own divinity. They take us beyond the sectarian chauvinism of organized religions to a universal, all-encompassing and unifying vision of reality and humankind. Organized religions in their present form often breed dissent and contribute to the global crisis. But a religion based on a genuine mystical perspective could make a real difference in the world.

L ASZLO: The other day, in Berlin at a symposium of the International University of Peace, the Dalai Lama said to me, never try to convert people to any religion. He himself, he said, never tries to convert people to Tibetan Buddhism. That is not the purpose—the purpose is the spirit that underlies religion, which is love, solidarity, compassion. He advised never to look to one religion to have all the answers. What counts is the spirit of religion, not the words of the doctrine.

There are cases and places where this insight is put into practice. In Auroville, the experimental spiritual community in India, for example, the founders decided that there is not to be any religion. Religious doctrines are explicitly to be avoided, the same as religious rites. There is to be just a deep spirituality in everyday life, reinforced by individual and collective meditation. When religion becomes institutionalized, Sri Aurobindo said, it divides more than it unites.

R USSELL: Many spiritual leaders have said this, and warned against their teachings becoming a religion. The Buddha told his disciples not to believe anything just because he said it. Only when it accords with their own experience should they accept it. More recently, Rudolf Steiner said that if he came back in a hundred years time he would probably be horrified to see what people had done to his teachings. Spiritual wisdom is a universal wisdom; but, as it is passed on from one person to another, each teacher's expression gradually takes on a particular set of doctrines and dogmas creating some very different religions. I am sure that if you, Ervin, revisited Auroville in 200 or 300 years' time, you would see that an entirely different religion had emerged in the meanwhile.

Today we are seeing a new spirituality coming about. It does not have a name yet; it does not really have a specific form; and it does not have any leaders. But there is a new perspective emerging which is very much in the tradition of the Perennial Philosophy that Aldous Huxley charted. Many people are beginning to rediscover the eternal wisdom of human consciousness and put it into practice in their own lives.

In some ways this is parallel to what happened with the

Buddha and his search for inner liberation. When the Buddha went out into the forest he spent six years visiting various teachers, tried many different practices and techniques until he finally woke up to the truth of how to ease the mind of suffering. Today we are in a similar process. But now it is not just one person; it is millions of us, all on that journey together, and learning from each other's experiences on the path. And the more we learn the more we are coming closer to the same truth. We are fine-tuning our understanding of spiritual development. I see it in the books I read, and the talks I hear people give— more and more we are saying the same thing. Maybe this revival will become another fossilized religion in time, but right now, at the end of the 20th century, it is alive and vibrant, and exploring that universal truth which is the core of all religions. That is why I find the current times so fascinating. We are in the midst of a new spiritual renaissance, but unlike previous revivals this one has no leader; for the first time we are rediscovering it collectively.

G ROF : I would like to mention here an observation from the study of non-ordinary states of consciousness that I find fascinating. We have seen repeatedly, both in work with psychedelics and in holotropic breathwork (which uses faster breathing and evocative music) that the experiences provide access to the entire spectrum of world mythology, to the archetypal figures and realms of all cultures. This includes experiences that come from racial, cultural, geographical, and historical backgrounds other than our own. It does not seem to make a difference whether or not we had previous intellectual knowledge of these mythologies. Modern people seem to have access to all the domains of the collective unconscious. This basically confirms the observations made many decades ago by C. G. Jung, observations that inspired him to formulate the concept of the collective unconscious.

People with whom we have worked in Europe, North and South America, and Australia often had experiences drawn from Indian, Japanese, Chinese, Tibetan, or Egyptian mythology. Conversely, during our visits to India and Japan, individuals whose background was Hindu, Buddhist or Shinto often experienced in their sessions distinctly Christian sequences. Over the years, I myself have had in my visions episodes with Hindu, Buddhist, Christian, Muslim, Shinto, and Zoroastrian religious symbolism, as well as African, Mesoamerican, South American, and Australian aboriginal themes.

This is quite remarkable! Many human groups have in the past used powerful mind-altering procedures including some that are the same as those we are employing ourselves—psychedelic substances, music, and various breathing exercises. And yet, their access to the collective unconscious seems to have been much more specific and restricted, limited essentially to their own cultural archetypes. For example, we do not read in the *Tibetan Book of the Dead* about the Deer Spirit that plays an important role in the mythology and religion of the Huichol Indians from Mexico, and there is no mention of the Dhyani Buddhas in the Bible or the Book of Mormon. So this permeability of the collective unconscious seems to be a new phenomenon characteristic of modern times. Had the collective unconscious been available to this extent in earlier times, we would not have today distinct mythologies specified for certain human groups and their religions. In the past, experiential access to the archetypes had to be fairly culture-specific.

In a sense this seems to parallel what is happening in the external world. In the past, humanity was much more fragmented and its various groups were secluded and isolated from each other. For example, until the 15th century, people in Europe did not have the slightest idea about the existence of the New World and, until the middle of this century, Tibet had only minimal contact with the rest of the world. Today, we can reach most areas of the world within hours by jet travel, there is a rich exchange of merchandise, books, and movies. And, most importantly, short-wave radio programs, satellite television, telephone, and the Internet connect every part of the globe with every other.

We are rapidly moving from a divided and fragmented world to a unified global village. And the unlimited access we now have to the archetypal domain of the collective unconscious seems to be an important part of this process. I hope and believe that this will provide a basis for a universal religion of the future. My idea of such a religion is that it would provide a supportive context for spiritual experiences and means of facilitating them—"technologies of the sacred"—but would have no interest and investment in dictating which of the many archetypal frameworks an individual should choose as an entry into the realm of the transcendental divine.

I believe that if organized religions are to become a relevant and constructive force in our global future, they will have to make their respective archetypes permeable, and accept that they *are* relative. This would generate an atmosphere of tolerance toward other systems that opt for a different symbolic form of worshipping the divine. It would connect religions to their mystical roots and to their common denominator, reverence for the Absolute, the divine that transcends all forms.

Joseph Campbell often quoted Graf Durkheim's statement concerning the function of specific archetypal forms or "deities." To be useful in a genuine spiritual quest, a deity has to be transparent to the transcendent. It has to be a gateway to the Supreme, and not to be mistaken for it. It should mediate access to the Absolute as one of the ways leading to it and not be an object of worship in and of itself. To make specific archetypes opaque and impermeable leads to idolatry, which is a divisive, destructive, and dangerous force in the world.

R USSELL : This is another aspect of the shift from seeing deities and gods as something "out there," separate from us, to seeing them as aspects of our own psyche. Increasingly we are seeing that inner awakening is not about practicing a ritual to some other being, but about working with our own mind. The question we are asking ourselves is how do I release my mind from the ruts it has become stuck in. How can I open myself up to the sort of experiences we are talking about.

G ROF : On the basis of what I said before, about the opening of the collective unconscious, I have a strong sense that the religion of the future will be experiential, honoring the spiritual

THE FIRST DAY · AFTERNOON

quest and respecting the specific forms it takes in different individuals. Hopefully, this religion will not be an organization promoting specific dogmas and objects of worship, but a fellowship of seekers supporting each other in spiritual search and realizing that they are all exploring a particular piece of the grand tapestry of the universal mystery. The awareness of the unity underlying all of existence and a sense of deep connection with other people, nature, and the cosmos would be the most important characteristic of this creed.

RUSSELL: Yes, and if there are teachings associated with this new spirituality, they will be about our own psyche—much as Buddhism is. It will be a contemporary teaching, and deal with things such as how the ego develops, how we derive our sense of identity, how we create unnecessary fear, how we interpret or misinterpret our experiences, and how we can free our minds from these various constraints. They will be psychological teachings, rather than teachings about deities and other such entities.

GROF: We had a very interesting experience at the 1985 conference of the International Transpersonal Association (ITA) in Kyoto. The ITA is an organization trying to bring together spirituality and science and work toward dissolving racial, cultural, political, and religious boundaries in the world. At the time of the conference, there was a serious conflict between American and Japanese businessmen and negotiations were going on.

One of the participants was the Japanese Jungian psychologist Hayao Kawai who had spent several years in Zurich, Switzerland, and knew well the Western mind, as well as, of course, the Japanese mind. He watched the business negotiations on the TV and laughed. He said: They think that because they have a translator, they are really communicating, that they understand each other. But they do not, because they are coming from very different perspectives. We asked him for explanation and he gave it to us using the Jungian approach.

They are coming from different archetypal frameworks, he said, and have very different metaphysical premises. The East has a model of the cosmos with a hollow center. Creation emerged from the Void as a total gestalt in which everything is interconnected, has its place, and ultimately is an equally important part of the whole. In the West, you have a cosmogenetic model that is very different. In the center is the source of power. It is God, the Big Boss, who created the universe and from this central powerhouse emanates a hierarchical system with diminishing significance. In the archetypal world, you have the tiers of celestial beings—from the highest ones, such as the seraphim and cherubim, through principalities, ordonnances, thrones, and virtues to archangels and then ordinary angels. And in nature, you have lower and higher organisms and ultimately humans, as the crown of creation.

Hayao Kawai explained that, in a dialogue between East and West, this difference in basic metaphysical assumptions colors everything that is said. It is like a discussion between Newtonian and Einsteinian physicists. They would be using the same words—matter, energy, time, and space—but these would mean something different within their respective conceptual frameworks. We found this idea very interesting and it inspired other participants to add some of their own cultural comparisons. André Patsalides, a psychologist from Belgium who had been born in Syria, gave a talk about the differences between the Arab mind and the Western mind. Karan Singh, Indian scholar and former regent of Jammu and Kashmir, compared in a similar way the Indian and the Western way of thinking. And Credo Mutwa, a Zulu anthropologist and witch doctor, discussed the worldview of Africans and compared it with the Anglo-American view.

It was fascinating to see how a completely new perspective emerged out of this discussion. We felt connected by our humanity, by all that we shared and had in common, and started to see racial, cultural, and religious differences as inflections and variations of basic humanity. They appeared to reflect the extraordinary creativity of cosmic creative intelligence that emerges from the underlying undifferentiated matrix. At the same time, these differences appeared as something very exciting and interesting, something that we can learn from and be enriched by. We were able to free ourselves from our idiosyncratic cultural programs and from the delusion that our own perspective on reality and our own way is the best or correct one. It was easy to see how arbitrary and relative they all were.

LASZLO: Teilhard de Chardin spoke about a process of progressive intensification or concretization, which he traced to the growing number of people on the globe, and to the increasing amount of information they are generating. It is possible, perhaps, that close to 6 billion people shall create, as you have maintained, Pete, a kind of global brain. I believe that this brain has an underlying dimension as well. It connects us in ways that our consciousness is not aware of, but one that on deeper levels we can tap into. Under the surface there may be an intensifying collective consciousness field becoming accessible to people in the altered state of consciousness—the state that Stan has been researching and of the potentials of which we have been speaking.

From Insight to Action

Healing ourselves and healing the world

L A S Z L O : The issues we have discussed this afternoon indicate that the basic precondition for creating a peaceful and cooperative world is better understanding between people, and between cultures. Are we suggesting, then, that the new spirituality is also a way of achieving intercultural understanding? Can spirituality enable people to live together? And beyond that, heal wounds in society and the world at large?

G R O F : The potential is definitely there. Transpersonal experiences in which we experience identification with others can lead to increased acceptance. I have seen it many times. The only problem is, can this happen on a large enough scale, and in good time to make a difference?

L A S Z L O : The people in Auroville, the spiritually based experimental community in India, are convinced that if you have a group of people intensely focused in one kind of consciousness, that will have an effect on other people, too. Do you believe that the diffusion of transpersonal consciousness is a real and promising factor? That this diffusion, rather than the spread of the new consciousness one by one to everyone, could make the truly significant difference in today's world?

GROF: I think there is that possibility! In India they believe that yogis meditating in the caves in the Himalayas can have positive influence on the situation in the world at large. And, of course, in modern times, we have Sheldrake's ideas about morphic resonance. Unfortunately, the concept of the 100th Monkey, a very inspiring and compelling image for this mechanism, turned out to be a fiction rather than a scientific fact. It created much excitement when people first heard about it, but then Lyall Watson admitted that he had made it up.

RUSSELL: Actually he did not make the whole thing up. The experiments were done, and were written up in Japanese scientific journals, as he stated, but the results were not as impressive as he made out; there was nothing that remarkable going on.

What I find most fascinating about the 100th Monkey story is how everybody flocked to it. People wanted to believe it, so much so that few people questioned its authenticity, or went back to examine the original research, which is most surprising given that it claims a quite remarkable phenomenon. It is the same with Sheldrake's ideas, which follow a similar theme—the idea that learning is contagious, and that the more people learn a given task, the easier it is for others to learn it, even though they may live on different sides of the planet. Again this is a pretty outrageous claim, but I find many people accepting the theory without question.

Why is that? I have asked myself. It does not seem to happen so much with other unconventional ideas. I think that deep down people sense that something like this happens; they feel it intuitively. There is a deep inner knowing that somehow, we don't know quite how, a person's state of consciousness can have an effect on the consciousness of others. We sense that some sort of transpersonal diffusion of consciousness does occur, and when someone comes along with theories or experiments that support this possibility, we feel that we have the proof we always wanted.

GROF: I would like to mention an observation that we could consider as indirect evidence. It happens regularly that reliving biological birth tends to open up access in the collective unconscious to images and experiences of unimaginable violence, cruelty, and bloodshed. People experience atrocities committed throughout the centuries—episodes from wars, revolutions, the torture chambers of the Inquisition, and concentration camps. When the process of self-exploration reaches this level, the experience becomes transpersonal; the history of the individual merges with the history of the species. People who began this process as personal therapy often feel at this point that they are actually healing not just themselves, but also the field of species-consciousness. It is as if the collective unconscious contained impurities, undigested stuff from previous ages, and as if bringing it fully into individual consciousness for processing actually represented collective cleansing and healing.

The depth and intensity of these experiences is far beyond the framework of what one can regard as personal and individual—people feel that they have become one with suffering humanity. Some of them refer to corresponding archetypes in the spiritual literature, such as Jesus suffering for the sins of all people or the Bodhisattva refusing personal liberation and voluntarily taking on the task of liberating all suffering beings.

This brings me to raise the question of the relationship between inner work and focused activism in the world outside. What is the best strategy for achieving an effective change in the external situation? I have already mentioned the yogis who supposedly help to solve the problems of the world without leaving the immediate environment of their caves. Years ago, Ram Dass and Daniel Ellsberg had a fascinating discussion on this subject at the annual conference of the Association of Transpersonal Psychology (ATP) in Asilomar, California. Ram Dass was involved in systematic spiritual practice and had some powerful transpersonal experiences. He came to the conclusion that the most important thing we can do to help the situation in the world is systematic inner work that leads to deep psychospiritual transformation. If everybody did that, the world would change. We would also avoid various misdirected activities that actually make the situation worse.

Daniel Ellsberg, an activist and pacifist who had exposed the secret plans of the American military circles by publishing the Pentagon papers, had a different idea. He was initially convinced that the only thing that can change the world is determined external activity—political protest, demonstration, boycott, and similar strategies. He felt that his participation in demonstrations, ending up in prison, and making newspaper headlines was the most effective revolutionary activity and the best he could do to catalyze positive change.

They thus started the discussion from diametrically opposite positions, but as they explored the issues deeper, they were gradually opening up to each other's perspectives. Ram Dass conceded that after we work through our personal biases and clarify our own position by deep inner work, it is important that we go and apply our insights in the world. Today he is deeply committed to service and dedicates much of his time and energy to environmental and other projects.

Conversely, Daniel Ellsberg realized that it is important for effective activists to do systematic inner work so that their interventions are fully conscious, properly focused, using skillful means, and free from the projections of their own unresolved unconscious drives.

RUSSELL: There is a definite possibility that a person who is working on himself or herself is having a direct effect on the consciousness of others. I know from my own experience that when I meditate with a group of people in the same room something happens—the quality of my meditation is markedly deeper and clearer. It is very noticeable, but not something I can explain except to suppose that there is some direct influence of the meditators on each other.

There is evidence that the effect goes far beyond the room in which people are meditating. Researchers studying the effects of Transcendental Meditation found that large numbers of people meditating together had an apparent influence on those living in the same area. They took teams of up to 5,000 meditators in a city and had them meditate together for several weeks. Then they looked at various social statistics for that city over the period of the experiment and found crime rates, accident rates, and hospital admissions decreasing. It sounds quite amazing, I know. But I don't think they are fudging their results. Critics have looked at the experiments and pointed out that the researchers did not control for this or that parameter. So the TM people repeated the experiments with better controls, and still came up with same results. It really is quite fascinating.

LASZLO: The internal/external connection is a very hopeful possibility. I have witnessed experiments on this in Milan, in Italy. There volunteer test subjects had electrodes attached to their heads to monitor their brain waves. It turned out that when the subjects enter into a meditative state, the two hemispheres of their brain fall into a synchronized pattern. The waves themselves are becoming harmonic.

Now, what is interesting is that a similar effect comes about when several people meditate together. Then the brain waves of all, or practically all, of the subjects become synchronized. An almost identical brain wave pattern emerges in the whole group, even though the people in the group have no sensory contact with each other. I have seen cases when, after five or six minutes, as many as 12 practiced meditators achieved up to 98 percent synchronization among themselves.

Synchronicities and curious connections

GROF: What fascinates me particularly lies in the purely psychological realm—in the realm of synchronicities, rather than of synchronization. When we do breathwork, it happens very frequently that people share the same experiences or that their experiences are perfectly complementary, although they do not have any contact with each other through conventional channels. It has often happened that people feature in each other's experiences, and after the sessions draw mandalas that are practically identical.

Russell: I don't think these synchronicities happen completely by chance. I have noticed that synchronicities occur more frequently when I am in a clear, centered state of consciousness. If I have just come from a meditation retreat, for example, synchronicities seem to happen all the time. It is as if the whole cosmos were on my side; everything works out just perfectly— much better than I could ever anticipate or plan. Conversely, when I am stressed, fatigued, and in an uptight or frazzled state of mind, very little synchronicity occurs in my life. So these connections seem in some way to be reflections of my own state of consciousness. This has the interesting implication that I can exercise a degree of control over the occurrence of synchronicities by tending to my own inner well-being.

Understanding these connections is tough within the current paradigm. Nevertheless, I have had sufficient experiences to convince me that the phenomenon does occur, and that there must therefore be something wrong with the current paradigm.

Laszlo: What we need is to realize that, on the one hand, these synchronous effects and experiences do occur, and on the other that they occur independently of any classical cause and effect relationship. Yet I wonder whether there is not really some kind of connection. When we do not find it, it is perhaps because we are looking for it in the framework of the old paradigm. Maybe we should be looking at individuals as parts of a larger totality. It is that larger totality that is undergoing a transformation, and the individuals are groping to understand what is happening—to them, and to the community and the culture in which they live. As long as we look for explanation in individual minds, we get all these paradoxical and seemingly esoteric findings. Whereas the real explanation may be on the level of the totality.

But it is important to clarify just what synchronicities and interconnections—or coincidences—we are talking about: those that involve different people's minds, or mind as well as matter?

GROF: There are two types of unusual coincidences that I am interested in. The first one involves simply a very improbable accumulation or combination of events. This type was first described by the Austrian scientist Kammerer, who was featured in Arthur Koestler's book, *The Case of the Midwife Toad*. Kammerer was fascinated by the synchronicity phenomenon. For example, one day the same number appeared on his streetcar ticket and on the ticket for a theater performance he went to see in the evening. In addition, an acquaintance of his gave it to him on the same day as a telephone number he had asked for.

C. G. Jung quoted Kammerer's observations in his article on "Synchronicity as an acausal connecting principle" and referred to an even more amazing story concerning a certain Monsieur Deschamps and a rare plum pudding. Monsieur Deschamps first got this pudding as a birthday gift from his friend Monsieur de Fontgibu. His second meeting with the same pudding was when, years later, he saw it on the menu of a Paris restaurant. He ordered it, only to find out that the last serving of this delicacy had just been ordered in another part of the restaurant by the same Monsieur de Fontgibu who had introduced him to it. He just happened to be in Paris and, "by accident," came to the same restaurant.

Many years later, Monsieur Deschamps had his third encounter with the same pudding when it was served at a party that he attended. The thought crossed his mind that the only thing missing was his friend, Monsieur de Fontgibu. Suddenly the doorbell rang and it was his friend looking perplexed and confused. He arrived for this third meeting with the pudding by error, because somebody had given him by mistake the wrong address. It is difficult for me to accept that extraordinary coincidences of this kind are just flukes—they are astronomically improbable. I tend to see in them the work of a cosmic trickster writing the script for reality.

Even more remarkable is the second type of coincidence, where one part of it is an intrapsychic experience and the other an event in consensus-reality, in the material world. Jung's famous example is the goldchafer beetle hitting the window of his study just when he was analyzing the dream of a patient that involved an Egyptian scarab. Joseph Campbell described a similar example of his own. It happened when he was writing his book, *The Way of the Animal Powers*. He lived at that time in Manhattan, on the 14th floor of a high-rise building. His study had two sets of windows, one facing Sixth Avenue, the other the Hudson river. He almost never opened the first set of windows since the view of Sixth Avenue was not interesting. As he was writing the section about the mythology of the Kalahari bushmen in Africa, in which an important hero figure is the praying mantis, he was surrounded by articles and images related to this character. In the middle of his work, he had a sudden impulse to open one of the windows that he usually kept closed. And there, on the 14th floor of a high-rise building in Manhattan, was a praying mantis climbing up the wall. What is the probability of something like this happening by chance?

I have observed that synchronicities become more frequent in the lives of people who undergo a profound psychospiritual transformation involving ego-death and rebirth. This experience usually results in many important changes in the system of values and the general strategy of life. People become more able to live in the present and with increased zest. They become less interested in rigid pursuit of specific goals. Their life stops being like a wrestling or boxing match and more like martial art. An even better metaphor would be surfing. If you are surfing, you cannot decide where you will go, you have to ride the wave. So instead of steamrolling their way to a future goal, fighting enemies and removing obstacles, these people sense where the energies are going, and how they best fit in. They simply go with the flow. It is very much like the Taoist *wu wei*, creative quietude or doing by being.

Life becomes increasingly effortless and, strangely enough, more creative, productive and rewarding. This is when synchronicities start occurring and unexpectedly support and facilitate whatever we are doing. What we are doing serves not just our own individual interest, but the benefit of the larger community. There is a sense of deep connection with others and need for service, cooperation and synergy. One feels appreciation for differences, increased tolerance, and a sense of belonging to the human family, to nature, to the cosmos. At the same time ecological awareness and sensibility increases considerably.

LASZLO: When seemingly different events in our own mind, or even in the mind of people we know, come together, we can always try an explanation in reference to memory and associative recall. But when an event that occurs in one's mind enters into a synchronistic relation with an event that takes place outside the cranium, in the physical world, we have to do with quite a different phenomenon. Here we need a very different framework of explanation. This is where the challenge becomes exciting for modern research on the scope and powers of mind and consciousness.

Personal Implications

The change in values

LASZLO: Yesterday we said that very likely there is an impending crisis in the world around us, but that there are signs of a transformation in consciousness that augur for the possibility that the crisis could be transcended. There are transformations under way both in the "objective" world outside us, and in the "subjective" world within us. Now in the latter, values play a major role. Just what is the nature and direction of the value shift unfolding in society? This, it seems to me, is a crucial issue, one that concerns all of us both individually and collectively.

RUSSELL: I interpret the current value shift in terms of a loosening of attachments of the ego. Our values are basically what we hold to be important, what is valuable, what we consider important in our life. In Western society many of the values have an element of self-centeredness and self-caring behind them. What do other people think of me? Am I getting what I need? How secure am I? Do I have the money, things, and experiences that will make me happy? Am I sufficiently in control of my world? These are the sort of issues we consider important, that we place value on, and which condition so much of our behavior.

As that self-centeredness begins to loosen its grip, which can happen as a result of the profound spiritual transformations Stan talked about yesterday, or as we grow more mature and wiser, there is a shift in what we feel is important; a shift in values. There spontaneously arises the ability to care more for other people, other creatures, and the rest of the environment. When more people get more in touch with a deeper level of their self, one that is not so attached to things for its sense of identity, we can expect to see a general shift in social values.

LASZLO: The big question is whether these changes in the values of individuals are powerful enough to change our institutions and our patterns of behavior. Because when one enters a social or professional role, one acts the way other people expect one to act. When, perhaps unexpectedly, one has a transformative experience and comes to new insights, there is a revolution in one's consciousness. Or does one go back and assume the same role and behavior as before? I wonder if most people really become different and act differently.

GROF: I have seen over the years many examples of people changing dramatically, not only internally, but in a way that had deep impact on their everyday lives. In many instances they remained in their old job or life situation in general. When one is a medical doctor, lawyer, or teacher, one can simply continue what one has been doing, but with a new consciousness, in a different way, with a changed focus. But there are some jobs that are clearly incompatible with the new way of seeing reality and it becomes impossible to carry on with them.

A good example is a friend of mine who is a physicist. He wrote a dissertation on the influence of the geomagnetic field on the trajectory of missiles. His dissertation was classified and he was offered work with the Pentagon. He told me that, one day, he and his colleagues were working on a specific task— how best to distribute the elements of a multiple-head missile to totally wipe out a territory of 100 square miles. As they were working on the mathematics of this problem, he suddenly realized that this was not an abstract issue. They were not talking about 10^2 square miles, but about human lives, mothers, children, families, schools, hospitals . . . He actually had a vision of what his activity would lead to. He got up as in a trance and walked out, never to return. He became a bodyworker and healer deeply interested in spirituality.

LASZLO: I, too, know of revelatory experiences that changed people's lives. Not long ago I met a man who is well known in Germany. When he was a young man he was a butcher and found contact with the US army headquarters in occupied Germany. He got a contract to deliver frankfurters to the Army canteens and became quite well-to-do in time. In the following years he built a large meat-processing company, specializing in sausages of various kinds. He became a rich man, with enormous slaughterhouses and several thousand people working for him.

One day he went on a vacation to the Sahara and spent two weeks living in the desert, very much like a Bedouin. Then it came to him, apparently very suddenly, that what he was doing was terrible for the animals, and not much good for people either. It appeared to him that his life was being wasted; butchering is not what he should be doing. He came home, sold his entire holdings, and created a foundation for ecological responsibility. His "enlightenment" probably involved an altered state of consciousness during his stay in the desert.

This can happen on the individual level, but for society as a whole to change, it should happen to many individuals. How can large numbers of people undergo experiences that have such meaning that they transform their lives? Is that possible, or likely . . . and can we do something to help bring it about?

GROF: We now have at our disposal many methods, ancient and modern, that can facilitate such transformation. The interest of the general population to pursue this path seems to be increasing. And there are many instances when such transformations occur spontaneously. Ken Ring described a man who was a member of the Mafia and was radically transformed by an

NDE, a near-death experience. Ken talks about "Omega experiences," referring to Teilhard de Chardin's concept of the Omega point in human evolution toward which humanity is heading. He includes among the Omega experiences, besides NDEs, also spontaneous mystical states, psychedelic experiences, UFO abduction experiences, and spontaneous psychospiritual crises, or "spiritual emergencies," such as Kundalini awakening.

Russell: Illustrating transformations that involve a large number of people, a good example in our own culture is the eating of meat. Only 20 years ago vegetarianism was unusual, and often considered a pretty cranky thing. Today it is quite acceptable, and most restaurants have good vegetarian options on their menus. Several factors have been behind this shift. Some people have changed for health reasons; some are concerned about the environmental costs of meat production; some are horrified by the way animals are raised and do not want to support that kind of brutality; others simply feel they should not eat anything they would not be prepared to kill themselves. The net result has been a steady shift towards less meat-eating— not a shift towards complete vegetarianism, but towards a more balanced diet. This shift in values is coming about because people are beginning to understand and think more deeply about the world.

Grof: Ervin, you asked how we can bring a major transformation to large numbers of people. To some extent it is happening already, in many different ways. There are various types of experiences that can facilitate the transformation and evolution of consciousness. As I said, there are Ken Ring's Omega experiences. All of these have a profound impact on personality structure, worldview, hierarchy of values, and life strategy. They may all be associated with shattering insights into the destructive and self-destructive course we are on. Sometimes the experiences include actual visions of the social and natural disasters and catastrophes that lie ahead if we do not change. A natural outcome of the Omega experiences is a sense of planetary citizenship, deep ecological awareness, and a universal spirituality of an all-encompassing nature that replaces the current sectarianism and intolerance of the mainstream religions. I feel it is important for our future to make knowledge about the "technologies of the sacred" available on a large scale through mass media and create support systems for those who have spontaneous transformative experiences.

LASZLO: But let me touch again on a question that does not cease to fascinate me: where do these extraordinary experiences come from? Are they entirely internal to individuals, are they internal to humanity as a whole, or is the wave of experiences that we witness today triggered by something that is even beyond humanity?

GROF: In spiritual experiences, we have usually the sense that we are connecting with a transindividual source—a higher power or higher intelligence. It can take the form of an archetypal being or transcend forms altogether. When the latter happens, it is then perceived as Cosmic Consciousness, the Universal Mind, the Tao, or whatever other name for the undifferentiated divine we want to use. In UFO experiences the source seems to be extraterrestrial intelligence, beings from another part of the universe.

There is, of course, always the question as to what is intrapsychic and what is out there. From a larger transpersonal perspective, what is perceived as divine is actually a higher aspect of ourselves and the extraterrestrial experiences are probably coming from the collective unconscious. As in the Hindu concept of Atman–Brahman, the individual psyche ultimately seems to be commensurate with all there is.

RUSSELL: I sometimes wonder how much the question of what is coming from within ourselves and what is coming from "out there" really matters. Indeed, perhaps the whole distinction between "out there" and "in here" is illusory. What is important is that the experience itself is valuable. Spiritual experiences are nearly always powerful and moving experiences, and in many cases they change people's lives for the better.

GROF: What we can safely say is that these experiences seem to be coming from a source that lies beyond what people up to that point considered to be their personal identity, beyond the "skin-encapsulated ego." And these experiences have, in turn, the potential and the capacity to radically extend people's limited self-concept far beyond the usual boundaries.

LASZLO: Perhaps the dichotomizing of what is me and what is not me, is not really a good way to phrase the question. Maybe what we have inside of us is also a part of what there is beyond us.

GROF: This is, of course, the basic tenet of many esoteric systems—the human being is a microcosm that mirrors the macrocosm, a microcosm that has access to information about the whole. As above, so below. As without, so within. We can find this principle in the ancient Jain concept of the *jivas*, in Hwa Yen or Avatamsaka Buddhism, in Tantra, in Kabbalah, and in the Hermetic tradition. In modern times, a similar idea appears in Leibniz's monadology, in the holographic model of the universe, in Whitehead's process thinking and, of course, Ervin, in your own conceptual system. All these models, ancient and modern, offer a radical alternative to a strict and rigid dichotomy between the inner and the outer, the individual and the cosmos.

LASZLO: Yes. In my view the human being is an integral part of the world around him or her, not really a separate being. This is new in the West. The discovery of the value of individuality was a European discovery of the Renaissance. The individuality of the person became valued as unique and different from everything and everybody else. In today's culture we still think of the unique individual as having reached a higher level of development than the more collectively oriented person.

Lately, however, we are coming back to the realization that the individual is not entirely separate, but part of a larger, more embracing unit, of people and ecologies in his or her setting. This realization does, of course, raise fears that the individual is just a cog in the machine, a neuron in a global brain.

RUSSELL: We should not necessarily see increasing individuality as a bad thing. It is an important part of our evolutionary development; without it our culture would not have developed as it has. What is important now is to balance this sense of individuality with a complementary awareness that we are also part of a greater whole. This is how we develop greater cooperation and coherence; by moving on to a broader more encompassing awareness, not by trying to curb what has been one of our greatest strides in evolution.

Rather than trying to hold back our individuality, we really need to foster its full growth. The sense of self prevalent in our culture is in many ways a rather limited sense of self. Many of us derive a sense of identity from what we have and do, from how others see us, from our social status, from the roles we play in life, the work we do, the beliefs we hold, even the car we drive. This has many drawbacks. A sense of identity that is drawn from what we have or do in the world is continually under threat. If the things from which we draw our sense of self change, or even look as if they might change, our identity may be threatened. We may find ourselves doing or saying things, not because they are the most appropriate things to do or say, but because our sense of self needs bolstering.

Paradoxically, this can lead us to suppress our true identity. We suppress who we really are in order to conform to social norms and receive the recognition and approval that makes us feel good. Rather than being true to our own self, people too often live out some constructed image of themselves, and as a result do a lot of things without really thinking about whether they are right or not.

L A S Z L O : I fully agree. Not individuality as such is the problem but isolated individuality—the individual seen as separate, even cut off, from society and from nature.

R U S S E L L : That sort of blind individuality is the problem. We need to find ways to help people become more free in themselves, think for themselves, and get in touch with the deeper wisdom that lies within themselves and express that in their lives.

This more-evolved mode of individuality is not in conflict with being a more cooperative member of society. On the contrary, it can enhance cooperation. If you moved beyond an artificially derived sense of self, then you have moved beyond a lot of the self-caring that gets in the way of true compassion. You are better able to see and feel the needs of others.

G R O F : The dominant worldview of the Western industrial civilization does not serve well either the collective or the individual. Its major credo is a fallacy. It promotes a way of being and a strategy of life that is ultimately ineffective, destructive, and unfulfilling. It wants us to believe that winning the competition for money, possessions, social position, power, and fame is enough to make us happy. And as we saw in our earlier discussion, this in fact is not true. In this regard, Western civilization is under the spell of a major delusion. Those who pursue this strategy are chasing a mirage. It is a loser strategy, whether or not we are achieving the goal we set for ourselves. In and of itself, it is incapable of bringing satisfaction and fulfillment.

Ken Wilber has an interesting concept in his book *The Atman Project*. He explored and described the specific consequences of the basic tenet of perennial philosophy which asserts that our true nature is divine, that, in the last analysis, we are identical with the cosmic creative principle. Although the process of creation separates and alienates us from our divine identity, the awareness of this connection is never completely lost. The deepest motivating force in the human psyche on all levels of our development is the craving to return to the experience of our divinity. This, of course, is an impossible task as long as we believe that we are body-egos operating in the material world. To accomplish this, we would have to possess and become everything there is.

LASZLO: Can you elaborate on this, Stan?

GROF: There is a story about Alexander the Great that illustrates this well. He certainly was an individual whose unique secular accomplishments would be difficult to match. He came as far toward achieving divine status in the material world as any human being can possible hope for. He was actually often called Divine Alexander. The story goes as follows: After an unparalleled series of military victories through which he acquired vast territories lying between his native Macedonia and India, Alexander finally reached India. There he heard about a yogi who had unusual powers, or *siddhis*, among others the ability to see the future.

Alexander decided to pay the yogi a visit and enquire about his own destiny. When he arrived at the yogi's cave, the sage was immersed in his regular spiritual practice. Alexander impatiently interrupted his mediation asking him if he indeed had the power to see the future. The yogi nodded in silence and returned to his meditation. Alexander interrupted him again with another urgent question: "Can you tell me if my conquest of India will be successful?" The yogi meditated for a while and then he slowly opened his eyes. He gave Alexander a long gentle look and said compassionately: "What you will ultimately need is about six feet of ground."

It would be difficult to find a more poignant example of our human dilemma—our desperate effort to seek realization of our divinity through material means and with the limitations imposed on us by our identification with the body ego. The only way we can attain our full potential as divine beings is through an inner experience. This requires the death and transcendence of our separate selves, the dying of our identity as a "skin-encapsulated ego." Because of our fear of annihilation and because of our grasping onto the ego we have to settle for Atman substitutes or surrogates. These change as we go through life and are always specific for a particular stage.

For a fetus and the newborn, the Atman substitute is the blissful experience in a good womb or on a good breast. For an infant it is satisfaction of the basic physiological drives and of the need for security. By the time we attain the adult age, the Atman project reaches enormous complexity. The Atman surrogates now cover a wide spectrum and include, besides food and sex, also money, fame, power, appearance, knowledge, and many other things. At the same time, we feel that in the deepest sense we are actually identical with the creative principle and with the totality of creation. For this reason, substitutes of any degree and scope will always remain unsatisfactory. The ultimate solution for insatiable greed is in the inner world, not in secular pursuits of any kind and scope. Only the experience of one's divinity in a non-ordinary state of consciousness can ever fulfill our deepest needs.

On goals in life

LASZLO: Let us move on now to a more mundane question, but no less important. There is a general loss of meaning in today's world. Most people do not know just what is really important in their lives. Perhaps we can shed light on this as well.

Let me start off by asking what is important in what we are doing just now—in dialogue. To my mind a key element of any dialogue, beyond all the techniques of putting people in the right frame of mind, is to make sure that the participants know what the others are talking about. They must understand that what is being said is important to discuss—that there is something to be understood which is not yet properly understood.

They must realize that it is more important to understand the viewpoint of the others than defend their own. If one can get beyond fondling one's own ego and understand that there is something to be achieved through the dialogue, then there will be more openness, more willingness to put aside petty concerns about "whose point is it anyway?" Focusing on the issue is what should count.

RUSSELL: We can apply that principle to our lives as well. What is really important in my life? Just asking the question What do I really want? can be a very profound exercise. The answers that first come up are often a result of our experience and social conditioning, or they may be constrained by what we believe possible. But if you keep asking the question over and over, going deeper each time, looking at Why do I want that thing?, most people arrive at very similar conclusions. In the final analysis we are all seeking to feel better inside, to be more at peace, to be free from suffering. We think that we want external things—money, promotion, a better relationship, a vacation—but these are all means to another end. Ultimately we are all looking to improve our state of consciousness. This is not to imply that one should give up work and just seek inner peace. But it is important to remain aware that work or money are not ends in themselves, only a means to a more profound spiritual end.

LASZLO: There are degrees of meaningfulness in the kind of work one is doing. The lowest level is when one just works so one gets a paycheck—it does not matter what one is doing. Obviously there are some jobs that need to be done that do not have much intrinsic meaning to them. When one is out of work, one is ready to do those things, too, but hopefully one day some of these meaningless jobs will be taken over by machines so that people can do the more meaningful things.

On the second level, there are things that we do because we are really interested in them, they are fun to do or happen to be a kind of hobby. It is nice when one can even make money out of one's hobby. That seems to be an ideal case, but it is still not the highest level, because doing this kind of work can be just an entertaining pastime.

On the next level one asks oneself, is the work I am doing truly meaningful? Does it serve some purpose? Does it lead to personal fulfillment? If one can find an answer to that, or if one can find the kind of activities that are both fun to do and lead to some goal that is fulfilling, then one is very lucky. Of course, sometimes the higher level goals are not easy to achieve. Sometimes they require sacrifice. Think of the martyrs—I don't think they go voluntarily to sacrifice themselves unless they are convinced of the importance of reaching their goal. Or think of great artists who live in garrets and sacrifice their everyday well-being just so they can fulfill themselves in their art. What level one reaches depends on how ambitious one is. But, unless one is really hard up, one should get beyond the first level. When one is only doing something just to make money, then one forgets about it as soon as the job is done. One closes the door of the office or shop, and starts looking around for how to spend the money the job has paid.

Best, it seems to me, is to combine one's private life and social activity in a way that is both fun and meaningful. Then one can be fulfilled at the same time as keeping body and soul together. It is important to dare to follow one's inclinations and follow the sense that one goes after what one wants to accomplish in life.

Of course, there is a catch here, one that is not present in everybody's life, but in a great many people's lives, especially in the Western world, and that is intrinsic skepticism about wanting to, or even being able to, benefit society and live in harmony with nature. I mean the view that all this talk about goals and meaning is to delude oneself—basically, people work because they want money. Ultimately, from the office boy and the street worker all the way to the president of the company and the president of the country, everybody is out just to make a living—and get rich if he can. This kind of thinking dismisses everything that is connected with meaningful work and achievement beyond the monthly paycheck.

RUSSELL: This brings up the whole question of why people are so attached to money. Money itself doesn't make us happy; having piles of green paper or bits of gold metal or numbers printed on a bank statement does not make for happiness. The value of money is in what we can purchase with it. We can use it to buy all those various things that we think will make us happy, more secure and more at peace with ourselves. It all comes back to the belief that how we feel inside depends upon what we have or do in the world, from the type of experiences available to us. The more money we have, the happier we will be. That is what we think. But there is actually very little correlation between wealth and happiness. I know wealthy people who are sad, insecure, worried souls; and I have friends who by Western standards are poor people, just scraping by with odd jobs, yet they are some of the happiest, kindest, most loving people I know.

LASZLO: They have escaped consumer society. All these money-making traps and incentives are telling you that if you have money you can buy things that will give you comfort as well as status and prestige. You are a better person the more things you own.

Not long ago, in India, I saw an advertisement for a product—a refrigerator, I believe—which simply said: "Owner's pride, neighbor's envy." If you buy this product you will take pride in it and your neighbor will be envious. That is considered to be the main incentive for buying it. This is the kind of fallacy that says that you are a better person if you can afford to buy a more expensive product. You can be proud of yourself, and your neighbors will envy you.

RUSSELL: If you look at just about any advertisement for any product or any service, you will find that the underlying message is, buy this and you will feel better. It is appealing to that belief that what you have or do determines whether or not you feel at peace inside. It is this belief that keeps us trapped, and advertising is doing everything in its power to reinforce it.

GROF: What fascinates me is the psychology of advertising. We all know how frequently the advertising people exploit pride, greed, and even sexuality to sell their products. The latter is transparent and obvious, at least for the better educated and more sophisticated customers, familiar with Freudian psycho-analysis, who can not only recognize when sex is used explicitly for promotional purposes, but also decipher more subtle hidden sexual symbolism. In her work on addiction and spirituality, Christina discovered that the advertising industry has been increasingly using spiritual symbolism to lure customers. Christina has a large collection of such advertisements, linking various products to gold, precious stones, divine light, star-filled sky, rainbows, peacock designs, mountain peaks, and other symbols commonly used in various spiritual traditions. This makes it very explicit that for the Western industrial civiliz-ation the material pursuit and the cornucopia of the market are surrogates for the spirituality we have lost.

RUSSELL: What is important about the consciousness revolu-tion we have been talking about is that people are beginning to wake up and recognize the truth, the truth deep inside us all that says No, that's not so; I have a choice about how I feel. I need not be a victim of external circumstances. People are finding the courage to stand up for that inner truth. And the more we each do that, the more we empower others to stand up for what they know and feel to be right. This is what the awakening is all about. It is about letting go of our attachment to the material world.

LASZLO: If many people would wake up to this then there would not be those advertisements we talk about, or at least there would not be so many of them. It is a self-fulfilling mech-anism, a vicious cycle. People need something, so they buy a product or service, then they are told that they have done something wonderful, so they buy it again, or buy similar things, whether or not they really need it. The power of this cycle can be broken only at the point where people come to realize that buying more things beyond a real need for them does not make them any the better or the happier.

The equation of material standard of living and quality of life is a false equation. One can have a marvelous quality of life at a relatively low material standard of living. One can have a high quality of existence without spending a great deal of money and using a great deal of energy and resources. There is a choice of lifestyles all the way from the choice of profession to the choice of furnishings, to the choice of friends. One can live in a simple, high-quality way, or in an ostentatious, expensive and boastful way. There is this choice.

In the Western world we live in an aggressive and competitive culture. But in the same Western world, as we have said, there is also a leading edge, an advance guard of people who are increasingly coming in touch with themselves and the world at large through transformative experiences. But the great majority have not gone through these experiences. They live a humdrum existence, framed in competition with others within over-powering systems, trying to hold their jobs and keep body and soul together. They are fed information mainly from the news media, from advertising and the public educational system. It is difficult for most of them to rise above this level.

Of course, in traditional societies people are generally more in touch with reality as it unfolds around them. But even there, many people are intent on achieving what they consider pro-gress along the Western pattern. This means that of the 6 billion people in today's world, not more than a few million are ready to enter on a path that could lead to transformative experiences. The great mass of people are still marching to the beat of a different drum.

Yet, unless a new consciousness can reach the bulk of today's people, we will be in trouble. No matter how much some people change in California, if people in China are not moving along a transformative path, they will just emulate what they believe are Western values and repeat our mistakes. And if conscious-ness does not change in the mainstream of Western society, they will be reinforced in this belief. We must not only preach to others, but do what we preach ourselves. Because it seems to me imperative that consciousness evolve the world over.

GROF: Several years ago, Czech president Václav Havel gave an interesting talk at Stanford University when he received the Jackson H. Ralston Award. In his talk he criticized the form Western democracy has taken in recent decades. He pointed out that it was originally founded on deep spiritual principles, but has degenerated into a sort of consumer strategy. The influence of the Western world on the developing countries consists primarily in exporting technology and consumer goods. And very frequently this happens at the expense of suppressing and destroying the authentic ritual and spiritual life of these countries and replacing it with materialism and atheism. In many instances democratic countries have used immoral and antidemocratic means to promote their interests. Havel emphasized that this form of "democracy" devoid of high spiritual principles is not much of a hope for our troubled world.

THE SECOND DAY · MORNING

LASZLO: People in the less industralized world look to us to see what is the desirable lifestyle, the nature of the good life, and they often get the wrong indications.

GROF: Modern technology can be tremendously seductive for traditional people. It offers many gadgets and fascinating toys that can make life more comfortable and easier, at least from a superficial perspective. Yet it has a destructive influence on the cultural life of the so called "developing" countries. Wherever modern technology is imported, it tends to destroy traditional values, ritual and spiritual life, and creative expressions in craft and art.

RUSSELL: The most dangerous thing we are exporting is our values. Through the products we are encouraging people to buy, and through the media—in particular television—we are encouraging those in the developing countries to adopt our self-centered materialistic value system. It is this mode of consciousness that is at the root of our collective insanity.

So I do not think it is a question of how we get the rest of the world to change its consciousness, but how can we encourage that shift of consciousness in the West. That is where it is most needed. It is up to us to set an example to the rest of the world.

G ROF: I absolutely agree. Exporting our system of values and our lifestyle in their present form to the developing countries is a recipe for global suicide. Think of the size of the populations in China, India, Africa, and South America! Instead of doing that, we should be concerned about increasing the percentage of people in our society who are already changing, so that they become a majority.

L ASZLO: There is a consciousness revolution under way in our own part of the world. But there is still this nagging suspicion—is it really fast enough?

R USSELL: I don't think it is. The question is, what can we do to promote change. I often hear people saying that other people need to change; that politicians need to change, that business leaders need to change, or that ordinary people on the street need to change. But if we lay the burden of change upon others we are neglecting ourselves. It is very easy to say "they" must change, but we must remember that we are also one of "them." I am one of the billions of people who need to raise their level of consciousness. Moreover, I am the one person on this planet I can take full responsibility for. No one else is going to change me for me. So I think the first question is, how can I evolve faster; what more can I do to change my own consciousness?

This is not to suggest that my responsibility should end with myself, but that it should *start* with myself. Responsibility spreads from each person into what I call his or her personal sphere of influence. Our sphere of influence is all those people with whom we interact in some way. It may include our family, the people we work with, our neighbors and social contacts. For the three of us, who are all writers and communicators in a wider arena, it would include those who read our books, come to our talks and workshops, listen to us on radio and television. But it does not include everyone on the planet. The presidents of most large multinationals do not fall under my sphere of influence—unless by chance they were to read one of my books. So when we ask what we can do to help others change, I think we need to think in terms of those who fall into our sphere of influence. What can I do to help these people on their own inner journeys?

GROF: It is certainly essential to start with ourselves. It is easy to live under the illusion that we have already arrived and it is the world that needs change. But then there is also the question that Ervin insists on—how can we best facilitate the transformation in the world outside ourselves?

We have already talked about the importance of changing the paradigm, revising some essential aspects of the worldview of Western industrial civilization, and making the existing technologies of transformation better known and available. I believe that an equally important task is to find better ways of supporting the changes which are happening already. I have mentioned earlier that Christina and I are interested in spontaneous experiences of non-ordinary states of consciousness—mystical states and psychospiritual crises. Here belong, for example, the awakening of Kundalini, death–rebirth sequences, the temporary dissolution of boundaries and the feelings of cosmic unity, dramatic psychic openings, struggles with past life experiences and similar phenomena. Contemporary psychiatry treats these states routinely by suppressive medication and considers them to be psychotic episodes, manifestations of mental disease. We believe that they are actually crises of transformation. If they are properly understood and treated, they can be healing, transformative, even evolutionary change processes.

Another fascinating frontier is alcoholism and addiction. As you know, we are now experiencing an incredible epidemic of these problems. In the transpersonal field, there is an increasing sense that they are expressions of unfulfilled spiritual cravings and represent a misunderstood and misguided search for transcendence. People who have a strong need for spirituality and cannot find the right way to it opt for addiction as an unfortunate surrogate. We know that the only programs that have any chance for success are those that include the spiritual perspective.

There exists a correspondence between Bill Wilson, the co-founder of Alcoholics Anonymous, and C. G. Jung. Bill Wilson gives credit to Jung as the father of the Twelve Step programs. He gives the follow-up on a patient whom Jung had treated. After a temporary improvement, this patient relapsed and Jung refused to continue therapy with him. He told him that his only chance was to join a spiritual community and hope for a spiritual experience. The patient joined the Oxford Group and actually had a transformative experience. He was the inspiration for Bill Wilson to start Alcoholics Anonymous.

Jung suggested that the patient's craving for alcohol was, on a deeper level, actually craving for transcendence or, expressed in medieval terms, for God. The correct formula was, therefore, *spiritus contra spiritum*, to combat the ravages of alcohol by a spiritual pursuit. It is possible that on the large scale, the right strategy in the treatment of alcoholism and addiction could actually contribute to the psychospiritual transformation of humanity.

Russell: We need to ask why people look to drugs of one form or another in the first place. We too easily put the blame on the availability of drugs, but that does not explain why people choose to use them. Drug abuse is a symptom of a deeper lack in our society. If someone turns to a drug for some inner relief, it is a sign that their existing lives are not providing the satisfaction they seek. There is a hunger for something else; for deeper meaning, for inner peace, for fulfillment, for relief from stress. But because our society does not provide the means to satisfy that hunger, people turn to alcohol, heroin, or whatever else, as a temporary way of relieving that need.

GROF: In a sense, the alcoholic and the drug addict are just an extreme form, a caricature, of the average Westerner who is replacing the search for transcendence by a large variety of material surrogates, addictions of a different kind.

LASZLO: For some people it is alcohol, for some it is sex, and for others it is fast driving or fancy lifestyles. Given that many of the values and resources of contemporary society are not satisfactory, people are looking for something that would give them a deeper sense of fulfillment.

The doomsday scenario—and beyond

LASZLO: Many of the things we have been saying paint a pretty somber picture of life, and the prospects of a better life, in today's societies. On the one hand, the better-off people in Western and Westernized societies are becoming saturated. They do not really need any more material goods than they already have, they do not need to worry about where their daily food is coming from; they have all the principal varieties of consumer goods. Many of these people are now looking for something else. This often means taking refuge in alcoholism or drug addiction, and lately also in an escape into virtual reality. The search can take people to the esoteric sphere as well, looking for spiritual guidance from gurus, mediums, or disembodied spirits. On the other hand, people who do not have an assurance of material well-being are looking more for material things—it is difficult for them to undergo transformative experiences and develop a higher kind of consciousness.

For those who already have a good level of material well-being, the next step can be to try other experiences, at worst alcohol and drugs, and at best, if they are wise, a transformation in consciousness. For others, the next step is usually just to reach a higher level of material well-being. But in that case the great majority of humanity would find itself in an almost hopeless situation. There are not enough resources in today's economic and technological environment for everybody to achieve the kind of material standard that those in the industrialized world have already achieved. Yet it is not enough only for the well-off populations to evolve their consciousness; the rest have to do likewise. If they just emulate the material lifestyle of people in the industrialized world, we are all in trouble.

RUSSELL: Perhaps we have to help them through that phase. Materialism and the worship of money may be a phase of development which a society goes through. The Industrial Revolution launched Western countries on that path some 200 years ago. Now we are arriving at the stage where we are waking up to the fact that we already have most of the things we need, we do not need to go any further down this path. Indeed that would be suicidal. Perhaps our task now is to help the developing nations pass through this phase as rapidly as possible.

LASZLO: The problem is that, given the environmental and resource problems on this planet, there is not enough time for everyone and every society to pass through all the stages of development, as we have done.

RUSSELL: I agree with that, and precisely for that reason we should help them to evolve faster. Perhaps they can get through the materialist phase in just a couple of decades rather than a couple of centuries. We can already see the acceleration in the speed with which developing countries are moving from an agricultural age into an industrial age and on into the information age. India went through its own industrial revolution in twenty years or so, while China is almost jumping straight from an agricultural society to an information society.

Whereas the West had to learn everything from scratch, these countries are making use of the technologies and practices that we have developed. They do not have to develop steam engines, airplanes and computers; we have done it already, and they are learning from our experience. If we can also help them see that there is something more to life and development than the pursuit of material wealth, we may be able to help them move more rapidly beyond this phase of development.

LASZLO: Or even leap over some of this phase. It is dangerous to pass through a phase which involves the kind of energy-intensive and wasteful lifestyles and production methods that we have adopted in the West. If they take their time passing through this phase even while putting the structures and infra-structures of the next phase in place, they may overuse the planet's resources and overpollute its environment.

GROF: We are assessing future trends with our current tech-nologies in mind. The prospects could change drastically if we managed to reorient ourselves to other sources of energy, particularly solar. I understand it is already possible to drive cars and fly jets using hydrogen instead of gas.

LASZLO: We could certainly drive cars using liquid hydrogen—I saw one myself not long ago, a BMW that looked and behaved pretty much like a normal car except for insulated fuel lines running from a big and likewise insulated tank at the back. Out of its exhaust comes a fine mist that condenses into pure water. But people in charge of developing this car tell me that it will be 50 years before the technology could be pressed into large-scale service—it will be that long before liquid hydrogen will be as readily available at the roadside as gasoline is today. They do not seem to realize that by that time it may be too late to make worldwide use of this new technology—we may have overpolluted the air, and triggered a number of crises, many of which could have been avoided by a timely switch to renewable and clean energy technologies.

GROF: There are rumors that developments in the field of alternative energies are blocked by the oil companies, and that some of the promising patents have actually been bought and kept in safes. It is hard to anticipate what might happen if these projects become a priority and get full support. It should not be difficult to develop feasible procedures using solar energy to convert water into hydrogen and oxygen and to find safe ways of storing these fuels.

L ASZLO: Clearly, we do have many practical solutions at our disposition and could research and develop many others, but we do not seem to have the will to use them and develop them.

G ROF: This is exactly what I am trying to say. The inconceivable waste of the insane arms race on a global scale, combined with our linear strategies—plundering non-renewable resources and turning them into pollution—complicate the situation. If we had another system of values and other priorities, things would be quite different. For example, if our strategy were cyclical, the way it is in nature, the Earth could carry a large population with much less of a problem. The capacity of the planet and the Sun to produce food is enormous; we could harvest the kelp in the Sargasso Sea, for example, and turn it into a large variety of victuals.

L ASZLO: What I am worried about is whether there is a realistic chance that the kind of consciousness that we need in order to do this kind of thing could become sufficiently widespread to change the dominant patterns of development in the world—the economic patterns, the political patterns, and the social patterns.

R USSELL: What you are asking is whether we can reform our society?

L ASZLO: Or whether our society can reform itself . . .

RUSSELL: I am not sure it can. It may be past reform. As I said earlier, I think we may be living through the fall of Western civilization. No past civilization has lasted forever. Why should ours be any different? On the contrary, there is every reason to suppose that it will eventually fall. It has proved itself unsustainable in the long term, and we are now coming face to face with that fact.

From a planetary perspective, ours is a rather crazy and very exploitative civilization. It would be hard to argue a case that we are a benign influence on the biosphere. If there were a planetary vote on the subject, if you gave every species a vote as to whether or not Western civilization should be allowed to continue, then I suspect that almost every species, apart perhaps from cockroaches and rats, would vote against us. The vote would be 99.9 percent "No": Western civilization is not good for planet Earth. It should die.

LASZLO: By dying, you mean that the people who now live in Western civilization would cease thinking, acting, feeling and living the way they do and develop into something else.

RUSSELL: Yes. I do not mean that we should die as individuals, but that our current mode of being should die. A new culture needs to emerge.

LASZLO: Out of Western civilization or in place of it?

RUSSELL: Out of the fall something new will arise . . .

GROF: Like the phoenix.

RUSSELL: Yes. I do not think we are going to avoid disaster in one form or another. It is too late. We have gone too far, and reform will take too long. We are rather like a crash-test dummy in a car. It is as if the car had started hitting the wall. In slow motion the front of the car is beginning to crumple and the dummy inside is saying, Oh dear, it looks like we are going to crash. I'd better do something. Maybe I should get out. Or maybe I can put the car in reverse.

But it is too late for that, far too late. We are reaping the consequence of years of wrong thinking. It is no good trying to change all that now. The question now is, how do we navigate our way through what is almost certainly going to be the most calamitous time in human history. It is not going to be an easy time. It's going to be very, very uncomfortable. But I do not think there is any avoiding it now.

GROF: Many years ago in Moscow I had a long discussion about ecology with my friend, Professor Vassily Nalimov, a brilliant scientist, who had spent 18 years in a Stalinist camp in Siberia. I found the time with him absolutely fascinating. His primary concern was not the nuclear issue. He foresaw a possibility that the United States and Russia could reach a peace agreement and dismantle the nuclear bombs. What he was worried about was chemistry. According to him many aspects of our life critically depend on the chemical industry and he could not see how we could fully eliminate the toxic fallout that has been irreversibly polluting our rivers and seas, soil and air. He was afraid it was already too late.

LASZLO: This is a global-level problem, in that we are changing the chemical balances in the whole biosphere.

GROF: We are doing it in many different ways, but Vassily thought the greatest danger was chemical pollution, which is enormous and cannot easily be reversed.

L ASZLO: As we said, life will continue, there will be new mutations and new species emerging. But species that have short reproductive cycles will mutate faster than we do and will adapt better. We are going to be on the laggard side of evolution.

G ROF: Many years ago, there was a fascinating movie, *The Hälstedt Chronicles*. And exactly this was the message that it conveyed: If we do something serious to the environment, it will be the insects with their short reproductive cycles and enormous adaptability who will inherit the Earth.

R USSELL: Another doomsday scenario is not an ecological catastrophe, but the plague. We are wide open to plague today. We have reduced our natural resistance to illnesses. Junk food diets, drugs, over-use of antibiotics, chemical pollution and other factors have weakened our immune systems. At the same time bacteria are increasing their resistance to the drugs we have developed. And they are doing so faster than we can discover new antibiotics. Some bacteria have developed resistance to almost every known antibiotic, and when our arsenal runs out, there is going to be very little we can do to stop them.

Furthermore, we are making it very easy for diseases to spread through society. If a new plague broke out in São Paulo today, it would be on the overnight plane to New York, and in every major urban area in days. A new disease for which there was no known cure could, if it also happened to be highly contagious, sweep through humanity very rapidly. It may not wipe out the entire human population, but it could decimate it—which, from a planetary perspective, may not be such a bad thing. A plague is often nature's way of dealing with a species that is out of control.

L ASZLO: That is how nature deals with a problem. A species that itself becomes a plague or a cancer will reach a critical threshold that will block its reproduction, or prompt it to commit mass suicide, like lemmings. But humanity has learned to use so many short-term corrective measures that these natural adaptive responses do not enter into play. If we are short-sighted we put on glasses, if we do not get around fast enough we make use of cars, trains and planes, and so on. In the long term we are likely to project ourselves into a major ecological catastrophe, while in the short term we seize on temporary alleviating measures and hope that we have solved the problem.

GROF: There certainly are not many reasons for optimism, but things can also develop in an unexpected way. We have been discussing the worst-case scenarios based on an extrapolation of the current trend. Here I have to recall again what happened with the Berlin Wall and the Soviet Union. Things that happened there were positive, and they were unexpected and unpredictable. There can be some factors and forces operating behind the scenes that work in another direction. For example, we already have bacteria feeding on oil spills. Maybe there will be some science fiction type of solutions that we cannot foresee—new strains of bacteria consuming plastic, plants bringing balance back to nature by cleaning up pollution, genetic mutations fostering tolerance and synergy, and so on.

LASZLO: Well, as we said earlier, if it was purely a matter of blind accident which way humanity develops, our chances would be pretty poor. As biologists well know, in accidental mutations the cards are loaded against hitting on a winning combination. If there is a real prospect of pulling through, it is because there is something other than accidental hits and misses guiding the evolution of biological species. Such a factor may be at work also in the case of the essentially cultural, rather than biological, evolution of our own species as well. Its effects can already be seen in the consciousness revolution, and in the value shift in progress in many parts of the world. But by themselves, these processes may not unfold fast enough. This is why we need to muster the power of the trans-formative experiences that could speed up the evolution of our consciousness, and through that the evolution of our values, our ethics, and our behaviors.

G ROF: I would like to mention an observation that I find interesting and relevant in this regard. People who in non-ordinary states of consciousness are undergoing the process of psychospiritual death and rebirth, pass through specific stages associated with characteristic themes. These experiences often portray scenes of extreme violence, unbridled sexual excesses including those of various deviant and perverted forms, satanic sequences, and messianic episodes. In the process of inner trans-formation, these elements are transitory and typically result in a powerful spiritual opening and transformation. In the indi-vidual experiential work, the greatest danger is an exteriorization of the process, acting it out in a destructive or self-destructive way. The extreme case under these circum-stances is committing actual suicide instead of just egocide—experiencing ego-death with subsequent rebirth.

People who experience these episodes often note their simi-larity to what is happening in the world—increase in criminality, violence, and terrorism, sexual liberation in its positive and aberrant forms, growing interest in satanic practices, and mush-rooming messianic cults. This suggests the possibility that humanity as a whole is undergoing a similar process of transformation. Unfortunately, much of it is externalized. If it could be internalized, rather than acted out in a destructive and self-destructive way, it could raise us to a higher level of consciousness.

L ASZLO: This is a hopeful possibility. But how do we enhance the likelihood that it comes about?

R USSELL: Let me mention two things that I think are important. First, we need to disseminate techniques and techno-logies that would help us to be more at peace with ourselves. It is no good trying to create peace in the world if we are still at war with ourselves. If there is fear and hostility within us, we are not going to be able to live peacefully in the world. We can give it lip service, but it will not become a reality. Finding inner peace is a thread common to all spiritual traditions, and it is going to become increasingly important as we continue to move into a world that is moving faster and faster, with more and more decisions to make. If we are wound up, angry, or just plain exhausted, we are not going to make decisions that serve ourselves or others very well. Nor are we likely to be healthy.

So one critical area is the development of ways that enable people to be more at peace with themselves. I do not mean that we have to develop these ways from scratch. Many techniques already exist in the world's various spiritual traditions. What we need to do is research which ones are the most appropriate and effective in today's world and make them more accessible.

The second key area is human relationships. The essence of a good relationship is clear, caring communication. But this is something that very few of us were ever taught at school or college. We learn it through a process of trial and error, and often far too late in life. What tends to happen in relationships between two people, both at home and at work, is that both want to feel loved and be at peace, but a vicious circle is set up that results in neither of them getting what they are looking for. If one person feels hurt or judged in some way by another, then the common reaction is to defend oneself by some form of attack. It may be very subtle, just a shift in voice tone or body language, or choice of words, or it may be more obvious. But the hidden intention is to make the other person feel bad, to make him feel hurt, judged or attacked in some way. Unless the second person is very aware of these dynamics and is consciously refusing to enter into the game, he or she is likely to respond in a similar way, sending messages back to the first person that reinforce the feeling of being attacked in some way. So the vicious circle gets set up. On the surface there is sweetness and light, but underneath there is mutual attack. Each person wants to feel loved and at peace, but is seeking to make the other person feel guilty and bad in him- or herself.

So one very important thing we can teach people is how to communicate in ways that do not trigger this vicious cycle, and how to break it if it does get established. Every good communication revolves around the question of how can I shape my communication in such a way that the other person feels loved and at peace. I know that when I have done this in some of my own relationships, the result has been quite magical.

GROF: An interesting mode of communicating that can help avoid painful vicious loops in interaction and gridlocks in relationships has been developed by family therapists. What one has to do is to formulate one's verbal comments in such a way that they consistently describe one's own feelings, rather than involving judgments and accusations. We keep the partner informed about our inner processes and reactions to various situations in such a way that it does not entail blame.

RUSSELL: Yes, that is an important part of it, but there are many other things we can do to help the process. In essence it is what the Buddha called "right speech." How do you speak in a way that you do not create harm and suffering in others?

GROF: When we lived at Esalen in Big Sur, California, Christina and I conducted a fascinating experiment. We organized an experimental educational program with a strong experiential component. It consisted of a series of month-long programs, a total of 30 of them, that took place twice a year. Essentially, we would choose a topic that we were interested in, such as Maps of Consciousness, Buddhism and Western Psychology, Holistic Medicine and Healing, Addiction and the Mystical Quest, and so on. We invited for each of them several prominent teachers specializing in the chosen subject. Throughout each of these month-longs, we offered regular holotropic breathwork, gestalt practice, Jungian sandplay, group process, massage, yoga, rituals, meditations, expressive dancing, trips into wilderness, and selected movies and videos.

The guest faculty in these events covered a very wide range, from pioneers in new paradigm thinking, such as Fritjof Capra,

Rupert Sheldrake, Karl Pribram, and Joseph Campbell, to Mexican and North American shamans, psychics, spiritists, Christian monks, sufis, yoga teachers, and Tibetan, Zen, and Vipassana Buddhists. This rich combination of intellectual and experiential input alternating in a random fashion turned out to be extremely transformative.

We found that when we participate for an extended period of time in a workshop specializing in one particular modality, we learn very quickly to play the game, raise our psychological defenses, and often succeed in remaining essentially untouched. On the other hand, being bombarded from different angles and from different levels by new and surprising information and experiential strategies seems to have a catalytic effect. Over the years we have received many letters from people who participated in these workshops and wanted to tell us that their month at Esalen was a turning point in their lives. I believe a similar model could prove very useful on a larger scale as an instrument of transformation.

LASZLO: We are coming back to our leitmotif: the consciousness revolution. The way to transcend the doomsday scenario, it seems, is through transformative experiences that evolve our consciousness and change the way we relate to each other and to nature. This possibility has many entailments and dimensions. Perhaps we can follow up some of them this afternoon.

World and Individual

About birth and development—on growing into a new world

LASZLO: At the beginning of this century, H. G. Wells said that the future will be decided in a race between education and disaster. We can see some analogy of that today, in the race between the new consciousness and disaster. This has major educational implications. How could child-rearing from birth onward be adapted to the world in which we live? How could the educational establishment be made to realize that we are facing a critical point, a threshold in our collective evolution? And that we possess the potential for mastering, or at least orienting, this evolution? In most parts of the world the educational establishment is highly conservative, it has a great deal of inertia built into it.

GROF: There are many things that could be done in the sphere of child-rearing and education besides introducing the technologies of transformation and efforts to change the paradigms. Clinical consciousness research conducted in the last several decades has shown that human thinking, emotional life, and behavior are powerfully programmed by our early history—not just by infancy and childhood which has been known from Freudian psychoanalysis, but also by our biological birth and even prenatal life. Humanity could be profoundly influenced

by improving the physical and emotional hygiene during pregnancy and changing postnatal practices.

There are good reasons to believe that the circumstances of
birth play an important role in creating a disposition for future
violence and self-destructive tendencies or, conversely, for
loving behavior and healthy interpersonal relationships. The
French obstetrician Michel Odent is writing a book in which he
argues that this perinatal imprinting has the potential to sway
our emotional life in the direction of love or hatred. He shows
how this can be understood from the history of our species.

The biological birth process has two different aspects, both of
them very important for survival, both of them mediated by
specific hormones. The stressful activity of the mother during
delivery is primarily associated with the adrenaline system. The
adrenaline and noradrenaline mechanisms have also played an
important role in the evolution of our species as mediators of
the aggressive and protective instincts of the mother at times
when birth took place in the open natural environment. They
made it possible for females to shift rapidly from delivering, to
fight or flight when an attack by a predator made it necessary.
This mechanism has become unnecessary, since delivering
women no longer have to fear external dangers. It is an evolutionary anachronism.

The other task associated with birth, which is equally
important from the evolutionary point of view, is the creation of the bond between the mother and the newborn. This
process involves the hormone oxytocin, which induces
maternal behavior in animals and humans, and endorphins
that foster dependency and attachment. Prolactin, the
hormone that is instrumental in nursing, has similar effects.
The busy, noisy, and chaotic milieu of many hospitals brings
associations with danger, death, and emergency and it engenders anxiety that engages the adrenalin mechanisms
unnecessarily. Like the jungle setting in primordial times, such
a situation calls for aggressive responses. It conveys and
imprints the picture of a world that is potentially dangerous
and interferes with the process of bonding.

Conversely, a quiet, safe, and private environment during
delivery creates an atmosphere of safety that engenders

affectionate patterns of relating. It creates a disposition for trust, loving behavior, cooperation, and synergy. Radical improvement in birth practices could have a far-reaching positive influence on the emotional and physical well-being of the human species and assuage the insanity of behavior that is currently threatening to destroy the very basis of life on this planet. This would be a good place to start.

RUSSELL: You mentioned, Stan, how important are influences in early childhood. This is another area where profound changes in humanity could be initiated. The knowledge that early childhood has a tremendous influence on the development of personality has been around for a century; it lies at the core of a lot of psychotherapy. But besides doing all we can to help people deal with the impact this has on their lives, and free themselves from some of the undesirable influences, there is also a lot that could be done to change the way we bring up children in the first place, so that they grow up to be psychologically healthier adults.

Like natural childbirth, there is already a movement in this direction. I have friends who had children in the late sixties and early seventies and who applied some of their changed views to the way they brought up their children. Things like not punishing their children when they made mistakes, but trying to help them understand; providing an environment in which there was the opportunity for greater emotional closeness; treating them as young human beings rather than dumb babies. Their children have grown up to be mentally healthy, well-balanced adults. They are now having their own families, and are treating their children in a similar way—or often in an even better way, for their awareness of these issues is usually much greater than that of their parents. The result is some of the most remarkable, bright, kind, caring, aware young people I have ever met.

There is a vicious circle here that is beginning to be broken. Children brought up in dysfunctional families learn a dysfunctional model and tend to make dysfunctional parents. Teaching people how to raise children in more caring ways can break this vicious circle, and can have a major long-term impact on society. Indeed, I sometimes think it may be the most important thing we can do for society.

GROF: But education is just part of the problem. It would take more than knowing what should be done. We also have to be able to do it. And that would mean a real emotional transformation of the parents.

LASZLO: There are, indeed, vicious cycles here, especially in formal schooling. Teachers are teaching what they learned themselves as students, and they are comfortable with that. It is very difficult to get radically new knowledge into the educational establishment. The people themselves who create such knowledge would have to bring it in, but they seldom move into a position where they become influential teachers. More often the people who have innovative ideas are not the people who are good at imparting and communicating those ideas. The educational system would have to be made much more flexible than it is today, much more open to new and relevant ideas, wherever they may come from.

GROF: Yes, our educational institutions have the wrong orientation and are teaching an outdated worldview. This helps to perpetuate and to reinforce the situation in the world. Take, for example, history. There is no appreciation for spiritual, transpersonal values. If you learn history, the important figures are Genghis Khan, Napoleon, Hitler, and Stalin. One does not hear much about the Buddha. There is a tremendous emphasis on conflict, fight, and competition—who wins and who loses. And, in general, negative characters attract and get an inappropriate amount of attention.

RUSSELL: Many of the things that we have been talking about would not go down well in the current educational system.

Mystical experiences, for example, are often seen to be very unworldly. Or educating people about non-ordinary states of consciousness would probably create a lot of hostility.

G ROF : Especially teaching something transpersonal, something genuinely spiritual, would run into a lot of problems. One would encounter resistance not only from materialistic scientists, but also from the organized religions.

L ASZLO : Yet the very fact that we can have this conversation and publish it is an indication that there is interest in these topics. Maybe ten, five years ago even, we would not have had this same opportunity.

G ROF : I am optimistic, or at least moderately optimistic, particularly if we consider that there might be some powerful factors operating behind the scenes that are not immediately obvious.

L ASZLO : That, to my mind, is a source of great hope. If there are such factors, they will make themselves more and more manifest.

But the immediate and urgent question is, how do we break through to reach not only the educational system, but the whole public information system, above all, the printed and the electronic media. For the time being that system is looking mainly for sensationalistic items, for those are the items that can be most widely sold. "Real" news is what is violent, or catastrophic, or what stems from the sayings and doings of a few public figures in the world. The underlying processes that operate in and shape the world simply do not penetrate to the public consciousness—they are not considered newsworthy.

Of course, if you want to look at the positive side you can say that we did not have all these television programs and news items on environmental problems, resource problems, population problems, development problems and the rest even a few short years ago. There is a real growth in awareness, yet it seems much too slow to give birth to a rapid movement capable of catalyzing realistically effective change.

GROF: In our culture, the media have enormous power to disseminate information and shape public opinion. I feel that we are approaching a critical turning point in this regard. In the past, there was a definite tendency to discredit and ridicule indiscriminately everything that was seen as "New Age," which meant basically anything challenging the established ways of thinking and doing things, from David Bohm's holographic model of the universe to nude marathons, crystal scrying, and pyramid power. Recently, there has been a significant change. Transpersonal books appear more and more frequently on the list of bestsellers and the number of blockbuster movies with transpersonal focus is rapidly growing. The publishers are getting the message that these issues are very relevant for people and that there is money to be made here. And the media people are astounded by the ratings of transpersonal programs, such as Bill Moyer's discussions with Joseph Campbell. Ratings speak a language the media people understand and respond to. Once they realize that this is something that people are really interested in, things could happen very fast.

LASZLO: But how do you trigger the rapid and timely unfolding of this process?

GROF: Enormous changes have taken place already. For example, the environmental concerns and the emphasis on naturally grown food that used to be seen as ridiculous hippie fads have become practically mainstream. This was not because somebody sat down and charted a brilliant strategy how to shift public opinion and influence the media. The trigger was the changes that occurred in tens or hundreds of thousands of people like you and me through a wide variety of mechanisms.

These people are concerned and are doing the best they can following their feelings. Each of them is just a grain of sand in the desert, but together they make a difference.

Russell: There are thousands upon thousands of people doing what they feel to be the right thing for them to do. And there is no single right thing. You, Stan, do your work. You feel it is the right thing for you to do, and you do it as best you can. So do you, Ervin; and so do I. We are all contributing as best we know how, and we are being supported by hundreds of thousands of other people who are also making their own contributions, doing what they each feel is the right thing for them.

The crucial question is how can we each do what we are doing more effectively, with greater impact? The more effective I can be in my own work, the more that facilitates change in others. And the more effective others are in their work, the more that impacts on me.

One of the most rewarding things I get from being a writer is meeting people who tell me that something I wrote in one of my books had a deep effect on them—like a piece in the jigsaw of life falling into place. And I am sure the same happens to you, Stan, when you get feedback from people who have been in your breath workshops. We are each of us pulling together the pieces that allow us to make more sense of our lives, and to lead happier, healthier and more caring lives. Each little bit counts. And sometimes, that new little bit can be the piece that suddenly brings many other pieces together, leading to a breakthrough or spiritual awakening.

If we think we have to change others, we are missing the point. It makes us think we are somehow special. It puts us in the position of being in command, of trying to control the situation. We are all part of the same groundswell. The most important question we need to ask is, how can I put my own life in greater alignment with that groundswell? How can I do my little one-hundred-thousandth worth to facilitate that shift a bit further?

LASZLO: What you are saying, Pete, is that by doing our bit, and doing it well, we can get an effective process under way.

GROF: I agree, but I would add that it is not enough to observe the situation out there and focus exclusively on external interventions. It has to be combined with inner work. C. G. Jung, among others, emphasized that it is necessary to complement whatever we do in the world with systematic self-exploration and probing of our unconscious psyche. He talked about the need to connect with a higher aspect of ourselves, the Self, and tap the wisdom of the collective unconscious and the spiritual resources that are available to us. The deep information and the empowerment that we receive in this process help us find the right strategies for our life in the world.

LASZLO: As we said yesterday, what you are doing in the "inner" affects the "outer." But, as we also said, if people had a better appreciation of the interaction between the inner and the outer, they would be more responsible in working with the inner and would then have better chances of success in the outer.

RUSSELL: Like both of you, Ervin and Stan, I believe that miracles can happen. But we can't *make* them happen, we need to learn how to *allow* them to happen. It seems that we can do this by developing the right inner state, the right state of consciousness.

We were talking earlier about synchronicity, and I mentioned how there seems to be a strong correlation between my inner state and the manifestation of synchronicities in my world. I cannot make synchronicities happen, they are, by their very nature, accidental, beyond my control and influence. But what I can do is to put myself in a state of consciousness that allows these things to happen.

The same may be true on the collective level. The more our collective level of consciousness rises, the more we are encouraging the possibility of unexpected miracles. We may have no idea what they will be, or how or when they will occur, but by attending to our inner well-being we may be able to increase their chances of occurrence.

L ASZLO: What you are saying calls to mind an experience I had in my earlier days, in music. When one is performing—it does not have to be for the public, one can do it for oneself—if everything works just right, works the way it should and not how you want it to work consciously, the whole performance falls spontaneously into a pattern. One cannot help feeling that one is part of a movement, switched into it. This is a marvelous feeling. One cannot bring it about by willing it, but there are things that one can do to prepare for it. If one is not properly prepared, it will not happen. But when it does, it is like "going with the force." Perhaps there is such a force and we have to learn to go with it. Can we teach people to do that?

R USSELL: I think so. From my own experience I know that what holds me back from being in tune with the force, or whatever you call it, is my own resistance, my own uptightness, and this stems from my fears. Fear is a very useful process when we have some biological threat, but in the contemporary Western world we have eradicated most of the physical threats. We are seldom attacked by wild animals; we don't often have to run for our lives. Most of the fears we experience are psycho-social fears that come from our conditioning, and our early experiences. We fear what others might think of us, of feeling insecure, of not being in control, etc. It is fears such as these that hold us back from living life fully, from being in the flow. Deep down we are on guard in case our sense of psychological well-being is threatened in some way.

One of the most important things we can do for ourselves is to uncover these fears, see them for what they are, and learn how to live without them. I find that the more I see that most of my fears are groundless, have no real substance to them, the less they interfere with my relationships, my communication, and the way I respond to others. The more I can let go of fear, the more I can live in the "flow."

GROF: The most important obstacle to that kind of openness is a history of traumatic experiences that lead to emotional and physical blockages, a kind of Reichian armoring that separates us from the rest of the world. There are ways of dissolving this armoring, freeing ourselves from these traumatic imprints, and becoming more open to other people, nature, and the cosmos.

LASZLO: Do people who undergo transpersonal experiences become better members of the community?

GROF: Not necessarily after one set of experiences, although even that can happen. I have occasionally seen a person's life completely changed after one powerful psychedelic or holotropic breathwork experience. But that certainly is not the rule. The probability of a positive transformation considerably increases if the individual is involved in a consistent and systematic personal quest.

LASZLO: Is what you find, then, that people need to have a whole series of transpersonal experiences, lasting over weeks, months, or even years?

GROF: Yes. I discovered the transpersonal domain through my clinical work. What I have seen repeatedly was that people started this process as therapy, because they experienced emotional and psychosomatic discomfort. However, after a series of sessions they suddenly discovered the numinous dimensions of their psyches and their primary concern beyond that point was a philosophical and spiritual quest for meaning, rather than just therapy. And that led to a whole new orientation toward themselves, toward other people, nature, and life in general.

A new map of reality?

L A S Z L O : Consciousness changes, new insights are emerging. All this raises a question I would like to put to both of you, since it is particularly interesting and important. It is about the concept we have of the world. As of now, it is highly fragmented, full of splits and gaps—between mind and body, inner and outer, man and world . . .

G R O F : What you are hinting at, Ervin, is the need for a comprehensive paradigm that could integrate our split perspectives, pull them together.

L A S Z L O : We have already talked about a paradigm shift in science, and now we could go further. What kind of paradigm is it that we can expect to emerge? What kind is it that we would actually need? Clearly, the new paradigm would have to integrate our current, fragmented map of reality. It would have to embrace the knowledge emerging in the natural sciences, especially in the new physics, and bring it into the context of the human and social sciences. Such a paradigm shift could prove to be crucial, since we live in unstable times, times that are highly sensitive to every "fluctuation," every input of ideas, worldviews, and values, no matter how small and seemingly insignificant they may appear in themselves. Under such circumstances another Hitler could arise, but also another Messiah. We have to be aware of the power of ideas and of the power that lies in promoting ideas, especially if they correspond to the great needs of our times. This means promoting those paradigms that could have a positive effect on humankind and the world at large.

THE SECOND DAY · AFTERNOON

GROF: One problem I see is that the basic elements, the conceptual building blocks, of the old paradigm seem very logical and obvious and are much easier to understand. The basic principles of Newtonian mechanics are not difficult to comprehend and they seem like common sense, since they are congruent with our pedestrian perception of the world. By comparison, the understanding of the new paradigm we could anticipate would require tremendous sophistication in a variety of disciplines, including higher mathematics and quantum and relativity physics. In addition, its basic tenets are counterintuitive, at least in the ordinary state of consciousness.

Look, for example, at your own work, Ervin. You have an extraordinary command of scientific knowledge and the capacity to bring together data from a variety of disciplines in a highly creative way. But it is very difficult for an average reader to understand what you are trying to say without the necessary background knowledge. So the question is, how to translate these concepts into ordinary language and present them in a way that can empower the average person.

LASZLO: I am a bit more optimistic than you, Stan, about the power and diffusion of the new paradigm. I do not think it is more complex than the old paradigm: it is basically very simple. We mentioned Alfred North Whitehead before. Now one of the students of Whitehead, a great philosopher in his own right, Stephen C. Pepper, has written a whole book on "world hypotheses," showing that there are just half a dozen basic world hypotheses, or ways we can coherently think about ourselves and the world. One of these hypotheses is the organicist one. It is that which is emerging today. In this worldview the world is like an organism. Not only are individual human beings like this, but the whole biosphere and even the universe. This is a very natural way of thinking. Once you start adopting it, things fall into place. I often have the experience that when you go after some new finding that does not make sense, you can shift perspectives, adopt a different way of looking at it, and then it suddenly becomes part of a larger pattern. Part of the pattern that Gregory Bateson was talking about—the "pattern that connects."

The organicist hypothesis seems like a very new idea but it is actually a very old one. It only comes to us in a new guise, a more concrete and reliable guise, provided by the new sciences. But it is not difficult to grasp. It is just that we have been educated out of it, putting in its place the Newtonian mechanistic world hypothesis.

G ROF : But don't you think that one of the problems is that the Newtonian worldview is to a great extent in cahoots with the everyday pedestrian perception of reality? It seems to be an obvious and logical way of looking at the world.

L A S Z L O : It seems so only to people brought up in the Western and the Westernized world.

G ROF : I have seen repeatedly that in mystical states people obtain direct experiential access to an alternative perception and understanding of the world. Transpersonal experiences have the power to awaken us from what William Blake called, with some injustice to Newton, "Newton's sleep." But I am not sure to what extent this new organicist model of the universe can really be convincingly conveyed through purely intellectual means to people who have not had any direct experiences that would point in that direction. Particularly when they have had a very strong programming to the contrary.

It would certainly help if the new ways of thinking could be linked to a mythological vision relevant to Western culture. This is an issue that Joseph Campbell was most interested in. He pointed out that when we study the cultures of the past, we see that they all had powerful mythological visions that sustained them and propelled them. And he wondered if it was possible to identify the dominant myth of a culture that we lived in, or if it could be done only in retrospect. The questions he often asked were, What kind of mythology are we living now? Can we identify it? Can it somehow be brought to the surface, so that we can get consciously ignited and inspired by it?

RUSSELL: Another problem the mechanistically trained Western mind has with the organicist model is that this model has a participatory quality. It makes us feel part of a living universe. Our reductionist models and our accepted common sense lead in the opposite direction—they separate us from the whole.

GROF: Many cultures were able to actually live in a participatory universe, where they experienced themselves as connected to and part of everything else. Yet the cultures that were able to do this also had direct access to transpersonal experiences in their rites of passage, mysteries, and spiritual practices. Those experiences were incomparably more available in those cultures than they are in ours.

LASZLO: Our fragmented institutions and ways of life are the sources of trouble. They do not allow us to have integrated, holistic, participatory experiences anymore. The crisis awaiting us will also be the crucible of the transformation of the Western way of experiencing ourselves and the world. It will show how all things are linked with, and depend on, all other things. It will validate another worldview. But how to get this organicist view to the public ahead of time, without having to learn it the hard way—that is the great question.

RUSSELL: Yes, most people do not want to look closely at what may be wrong with our current model. They do not let go of cherished beliefs and behavior patterns until forced to, but by then it may be too late.

A similar thing happens on the personal level. A person leading an unhealthy lifestyle may be told by the doctor to cut down on smoking, change the diet, exercise more, or whatever.

But if people do not see any sign of a problem they are liable to ignore the advice. They see no need to change. Until, that is, something goes wrong. They may have a heart attack, develop cancer, have some other illness that forces them to listen to what they have been told for the previous ten years. So long as life is comfortable we don't want to do anything that is going to inconvenience us too much. It is only when things get bad that we accept the need for change. So perhaps we should hope that we do have a crisis soon; enough of a crisis to wake us up, but not so major as to destroy us.

L ASZLO: That is a difficult thing to bring about in the real world.

R USSELL: Well, I am not saying we should try to bring it about, only making the point that we may not come to our senses until things get bad. Of course, not everyone waits to get sick to change; there are people who do listen to advice and do change before things get bad, and that is what we need to encourage on the global level.

L ASZLO: I agree. But that only underscores the urgency of a new way of looking at ourselves and the world—a new map of reality. Stan, in your own books you talk about a new cartography of the mind. Does that not imply also a new cartography of the cosmos? If the mind has surprising elements and if it is linked with the cosmos, then the cosmos, too, must have some unusual elements. A different cartography than the standard one.

G ROF: The new, vastly extended map of the psyche that I have been talking and writing about is, at the same time, a new map of reality, since the two categories of experiences that it adds to the traditional cartography are not seen as pathological distortions, but authentic aspects and realms of existence. The content of the experiences in the first of these categories is the world as we know it in everyday life, but perceived from a radically different perspective. Instead of experiencing its various elements as objects, we *become* them. And, strangely enough, by becoming them we gain access to entirely new information about them. This is a radically different way of acquiring knowledge about the universe—not by registering different aspects of the objects of our enquiry through our senses and analyzing and synthesizing this information, but by becoming these objects.

The content of the experiences in the second of the new categories is even more surprising. It involves dimensions of reality of which Western industrial civilization denies the existence. I am talking about the mythological dimension of existence, the archetypal beings and realms that the ancient and native cultures considered to be divine. And yet, when we experience them, they are equally real or even more real than our everyday experience of the material world. They, too, can provide new and accurate information that we did not have before.

L A S Z L O : It appears that through such experiences we obtain an entirely new mapping of reality.

G R O F : Indeed. We are really talking here about C. G. Jung's collective unconscious, or at least one important aspect of it. The second aspect is the historical domain of the collective unconscious that contains the record of the entire history of humanity. Jung is not always clear concerning the archetypal domain. Initially he saw it as something that is inborn and wired into the hardware of the brain, not unlike the disposition to instinctual behavior. At other times he referred to it as the cultural inheritance of humanity. Later he started seeing the archetypes as primordial cosmic patterns supraordinate to consensus reality.

Observations from the study of non-ordinary states of consciousness bring strong support for this third alternative. They suggest that the archetypal domain is situated between concensus reality and the undifferentiated consciousness of the cosmic creative principle. It forms and informs the dynamics of the material world. For example, the archetype of the Great Mother Goddess is like a universal template that finds specific expression in individual mothers.

I am thinking here about the ongoing philosophical debate between the nominalists and the realists concerning Platonic ideas. The nominalists see them as abstractions from a large number of concrete objects that alone are real, whereas the realists believe that there is actually a domain where the Platonic ideas have an existence of their own. Non-ordinary states clearly support the belief of the realists. There is no doubt that in these states the world of archetypes can be experienced in a very convincing way. We can visit many different archetypal domains that are populated by mythological beings in the same way the world of matter is populated by humans, animals, and plants. The archetypal beings seem to exist on much higher energetic levels and have about them a distinct aura of numinosity. It seems obvious that they belong to a higher order, but they influence events on our level. This is why ancient and aboriginal cultures regarded them as deities. It is a very understandable attitude.

L A S Z L O : Can you give some examples closer to our own time, Stan?

G R O F : Years ago, there was an interesting movie about Jason and the Argonauts and their search for the golden fleece. This movie unfolded on two different levels. One of them was the material world where Jason and his crew experienced a variety of adventures. The other was the world of the Olympian gods and goddesses that had a dynamic of its own—conflicts, tensions, love affairs, and so on. These two levels were clearly interconnected. The deities had their spheres of influence on Earth and their favorites and enemies among humans. The agenda of the gods then projected into the events in the material world, confronting the human protagonists with storms, dangerous animals, and other challenges—or, conversely, bringing various fortunate turns of destiny.

This is similar to the concepts that underlie the best of astrology. The idea there is that our intrapsychic events, as well as happenings in the world, are an expression of archetypal dynamics which, in turn, is correlated with the movements and positions of the planets. Because the planets are visible, we can infer from them what is happening in the world of archetypes and, indirectly, what qualities of energies we can expect in the material realm. The relationship is synchronistic and has nothing to do with causality. This is why materialistic scientists, who think strictly in terms of cause and effect, have such a hard time accepting the possibility that there might be some value in astrology.

L A S Z L O : There is an element in the thought of Jung which is going in this direction. As we well know, Jung formulated his concept of the archetype in collaboration with Wolfgang Pauli. He was struck by the fact that while his own research into the human psyche led to an encounter with such "irrepresentables" as the archetypes, research in quantum physics had likewise led to "irrepresentables": the micro-particles of the physical universe, entities for which no complete description appeared possible. Jung concluded that when the existence of two or more irrepresentables is assumed, there is always the possibility that it may not be a question of two or more factors but of only one. According to him the common single factor that underlies and connects the worlds of physics and of psychology is the *unus mundus*. This means that the realms of mind and of matter—of *psyche* and *physis*—are complementary aspects of the same transcendental reality of the unitary *unus mundus*. Archetypes are fundamental dynamic patterns whose various representations characterize both mental and physical processes. In the mental realm they organize images and ideas; in the physical realm they organize the structures and transformations of matter and energy. Yet the fundamental reality is the *unus mundus*, and this in itself is neither psychic nor physical: it stands above, or lies beyond, both of these realms. This, of course, recalls David Bohm's more recent idea of the implicate order. That, too, is a transcendent realm beyond space and time where all things are given together. It is only our interaction with the explicate order, the order that "unfolds" in space and time that separates them.

GROF: Similar concepts exist also in Whitehead's process philosophy. The entire past of the universe enters into each new moment, each actual occasion, as part of causal efficiency. Whitehead also takes into account God and the realm of what he calls eternal objects. Are you familiar with Rick Tarnas' recent book *The Passion of the Western Mind* ?

LASZLO: I am. Rick is describing the history of European thought, showing that there was an ongoing discussion about the relationship between two levels of reality, the familiar experiential one, and the archetypal, platonic, or higher reality. By the way, he is also showing that the course of European history exhibits systematic correlations with planetary positions. For example, Uranus was always involved in breakthroughs made by the major Promethean figures, such as Newton, Descartes, Freud, Jung, and Darwin.

RUSSELL: Does this correlation allow astrological predictions about the timing of the breakthroughs?

GROF: It makes it possible to make archetypal predictions concerning the quality of the energies involved, but not concrete predictions. This allows a certain degree of creativity and playfulness, while the archetypes remain true to their specific nature. For example, we are now moving into a triple conjunction involving Uranus, Neptune, and Jupiter. In astrological terms, Uranus is related, among others, to breakthroughs and revolutionary changes of a Promethean nature. Neptune is correlated with the dissolution of boundaries and with mystical awareness.

Jupiter, in turn, tends to expand and magnify everything that it comes into a relation with. One could thus predict, for example, that this combination of astrological archetypal energies will be expressed as a major spiritual revolution of an oceanic nature, involving the dissolution and transcendence of boundaries. The removal of the Berlin Wall and the unification of Germany, the liberation of Eastern Europe, and the dissolution of the Soviet superpower were the first indications of this archetypal influence.

This is very different from the revolutions of the 1960s, which also took place during a triple conjunction, but with Pluto instead of Neptune. Pluto is Dionysian energy, related to sex, death, and rebirth and involves powerful dynamic forces. The revolutionary impulse had a different quality and resulted in violent clashes with the police and other authories.

I should add that Rick Tarnas also wrote a little booklet on the role of Uranus in scientific, artistic, and societal revolutions, called *Prometheus the Awakener*. He discusses, for example, Einstein's Uranus transit at the beginning of this century, when in one year he wrote three papers that revolutionized physics, and compares them with the Saturn transit over the same part of Einstein's chart at the time when he had theoretical arguments with Niels Bohr and had a conservative attitude toward the development of quantum physics. Darwin had a similar Uranus transit when his ship HMS *Beagle* reached the Galapagos Islands and he had the sudden revelation concerning the evolution of species.

LASZLO: There are correlations in the natural world that boggle the mind. There appear to be highly subtle forces and energies operating in nature of which we have no empirical knowledge yet, though we seem to have symbolic knowledge.

GROF: The astrological worldview itself does not specifically refer to forces; it sees reality in terms of synchronistic arrangements rather than causal connections. It points to a grand vision of the cosmos as a unified, orderly interconnected system reflecting an underlying master blueprint designed by a superior intelligence.

R USSELL: I don't know much about astrology as it is practiced today, but I am interested in how the ancients saw the sky and the roots of astrology. For many years I have been fortunate to live in an area of England where there is very little pollution from the light emanating from roads and cities, and consequently there is a good view of the night sky. As a result I have become very much aware of the movements of the planets relative to the background stars.

My view of the sky is essentially the same as that of people thousands of years ago, except that they had far darker skies than we do. When the Sun had set there was no light pollution at all, and the air was much cleaner, so the stars would have been much brighter. People also had more reason to observe them. There was no television, no movie theaters, no computers or even books to occupy their attention. For half the time there was only the night sky—brilliant and totally captivating.

As I watched the movements of the planets I noticed that significant events in my own life seemed to correlate with interesting configurations in the sky. I had one such event recently when the moon was midway between Jupiter on the one side, and Mars and Venus, which were in conjunction, on the other side, while Saturn was rising in the East. I do not know whether there is a cause–effect relationship between the pattern in the sky and my life; it seems to be more of a synchronicity, an acausal but nevertheless meaningful relationship.

I wonder, is this where astrology came from? The ancients must have watched how from time to time the planets lined up in the sky creating interesting configurations. Did they also observe correlations between these patterns and events in their own lives? If so, it seems only natural that they should begin charting those patterns to predict future alignments and correlations.

GROF: I find it unlikely and indeed hard to believe that astrology developed by a gradual accumulation of data generated by individual astronomical observations and by attempts to correlate them with historical events and human experiences. I strongly suspect that the discovery came in its totality, as an illuminating vision of a higher order linking the movements of the planets to archetypes and to inner and outer events. There exist many examples of such revealing insights in the history of creativity.

But since we talk about the heavens and celestial bodies, have you ever thought about that amazing coincidence: that the diameters of the Sun and the Moon combined with their distances from the Earth make them appear to be approximately the same size? This makes possible such a spectacular and unforgettable event as the total eclipse. Have you ever experienced it? Christina gave me for my 60th birthday a cruise of the Hawaiian Islands designed specifically for the observation of the total eclipse, and it was absolutely incredible.

I had seen some partial solar eclipses earlier in my life. I looked at the Sun through a film or a glass plate covered with soot and saw that a part of it was missing, as if it had been bitten off. Not very spectacular. But the total solar eclipse is not just an increment on the same continuum on which you have the partial one. It is absolutely different, in a category of its own. Even an 80 percent eclipse does not give a sense of what is coming. But once you are hit with what is called "the diamond ring" and the eclipse becomes total, you are catapulted into an entirely different reality. I found it impossible to relate to it as a natural phenomenon, it became pure magic. We were on a ship with several hundred people, and many of them drank Bloody Marys at seven o'clock in the morning and engaged in all kinds of inane forms of entertainment on the deck. But when the eclipse began, they were touched by it in the most powerful way.

What one usually hears is that ancient and primitive cultures reacted so strongly to eclipses because they did not understand what was happening. But here we knew exactly what was coming, when, and why. We had lectures by a professional astronomer who thoroughly prepared us for the event. And it still was awesome and shattering!

L ASZLO: What is amazing to me is how often people fail to respond to natural phenomena that happen quite frequently. For example, crimson sunsets and striking views of the moon. These are truly fantastic sights, yet people mostly disregard them. Think of it: here we are on a planet, and all of a sudden we see our Sun sort of dipping down beyond the horizon. If you think of it in these terms you cannot help being amazed, instead of thinking, well, it is just the Sun, doing what it does every day. How can people go about their business when there are such extraordinary natural sights? Of course, artists notice. But most other people do not.

G ROF: One thing that we used to see in our psychedelic work and that we still observe after powerful sessions of holotropic breathwork is what we call "afterglow." It can last hours, days, or even weeks. During this time, the perception of the world is radically transformed—the environment looks more beautiful, colors are richer and brighter, music sounds different, and lovemaking is better. Touch, smell, and taste are highly sensitized and zest in life is increased. Blake and after him Aldous Huxley talked about this phenomenon as "cleansing the doors of perception."

On the potential of art and the responsibility of artists

L ASZLO: We are touching now on faculties that are typically exhibited by artists and other sensitive and creative people. An intriguing question is, whether an artist—a poet, or a painter or a musician—can contribute to opening up the kind of sensitivities required today in such a way that the evolution of people's consciousness is facilitated? If he or she can, there is, or so it seems to me, a social and human responsibility entailed by the creation of works of art. This, of course, is an age-old problem. On the one hand there is *l'art pour l'art*, art purely for its own sake, and on the other hand the consideration of what art can do for the individual, and even for humanity.

GROF: This latter definitely does imply responsibility for artists, but we should also not forget that it takes a certain kind of audience to appreciate what the artist has to offer, and to value and support artistic activity in general. The artist is just one part of the equation; the other part is the sensitivity and receptivity of the audience. And that needs to be cultivated. I find it very disturbing how little humanities and particularly art are valued in this country. They are the first to be sacrificed every time there is not enough money. We need a shift in our educational focus to facilitate the development of audiences and to foster and cultivate individual creativity.

RUSSELL: In our society you are not taught how to appreciate art, or how to listen to music. You are presented with art, and you either like it or you don't. You are not given an in-depth course in artistic appreciation that could help you see what artists are doing and why their work is important. Artists may be putting their heart and soul into creating something that for them has profound significance, but we don't know how to understand or appreciate what they are trying to share.

LASZLO: There is always the sender and the receiver even if the two tend to fuse in actual experience. The receiver who "re-creates" a work of art through his or her perception of it is also an artist in a sense. Yet there is a tendency in the contemporary world to remove art and the whole world of art from the public. Art is reserved for a small coterie of initiates.

GROF: Ervin, in your book *The Creative Cosmos* you quoted the composer Schoenberg as saying that a true work of art is not for everyone, and a work that is actually for everyone is not art.

LASZLO: Indeed, Schoenberg and many other artists think in *l'art pour l'art* terms. Not all of them, but there are schools that are introverted and have no commitment other than to their own field. Art, they say, has its own laws, it has an obligation only to itself. Yet art is also an element in human culture, and could be an element of cultural transformation as well. I believe that the community of artists must have a role in this, just like the community of scientists and educators.

RUSSELL: Artists do have a role already.

LASZLO: But do they take it seriously enough?

RUSSELL: I think most artists do take their work very seriously. Why else would many of them choose to continue with such little financial reward?

LASZLO: I don't mean taking seriously what they are doing, but taking seriously their role in facing the tremendous challenge which we have been talking about—their potential as a catalyst for cultural evolution.

RUSSELL: I am sure some do. And I am sure there are many who do not see their work in terms of changing consciousness on a global level. Nevertheless, I believe most artists are serious in their commitment to what they are doing. Whether they are doing this from the context of cultural transformation or not, does not seem important to me. What is important is that they are doing what they are deeply drawn toward. Each in their own way is helping to push consciousness forward.

LASZLO: Great art, in principle and almost by definition, is one which grasps and conveys some form of insight, not necessarily a rational insight as in science, but one that makes use of the sensitivity of artists to understand their world. Thanks to their highly developed sensitivity, artists extend an "antenna" to the world around them and receive its mood, spirit, and dominant tenor—or significant deviations from it. But artists are not only experiencers, they are also communicators. Consequently their role and responsibility extends beyond their own inner world, to the wider world shared by others around them. Their public is potentially everyone who is a full-fledged human being, since every human being could benefit from the esthetic vision through which artists grasp the experience of their times.

GROF: When we look at the history of creativity, in general, and its most remarkable forms, in particular, we see that visionary states play an extremely important role. This is true not only for art and religion, but also for the hard sciences, including chemistry, physics, and even mathematics. Willis Harman wrote a remarkable book called *Higher Creativity*, in which he described many examples illustrating this. True art is not "human-made" in the ordinary sense, but comes from deeper spiritual sources.

RUSSELL: Are you saying that art is coming from a transcendental level of consciousness?

GROF: Yes, at least the best of it. For this reason, artists can provide in their art a bridge for other people leading to the transcendental domain. The mechanism would be similar to that in the Zen koan or in Tibetan mandalas. To create a koan or a mandala, the teacher has to be in a special state of consciousness. And their creation can in turn mediate access to that state by others.

LASZLO: It seems to me that it would be important for artists to become aware of this potential of their art.

RUSSELL: Why? Would they do anything different? If artists are expressing their soul, does it make a difference if they become aware of its impact or not? They are still going to express their soul in the same way.

LASZLO: I am not thinking in quite those terms. If artists become aware of the critical nature of the situation in which they and their contemporaries find themselves, and recognize the potential of art to catalyze the currently much needed deepening and evolution of consciousness, then out of their humanism and their sense of solidarity and commitment will come a kind of art that is more focused and oriented in a direction favorable to individual and collective well-being and development.

RUSSELL: I wonder, though, whether that will produce great art.

LASZLO: That depends on the definition of "great." I am not calling for art that is commanded "from above," like socialist realism or propaganda art, but for a sense of commitment by the artists themselves. This was exhibited by artists such as Balzac, Dürenmatt, Ionesco, and Picasso, among others. Other artists have a sense of commitment only to their own art, and that is as far as they go. But today that is not far enough. As we just said, art is an element of culture and culture is an element of the human community, and the human community needs a new consciousness. Thus also in regard to the evolution of today's consciousness, society needs art.

RUSSELL: This comes back to one of the basic themes of our discussion. Change comes as a result of personal experience, and that might be some non-ordinary state of consciousness, a person's experience of life, or some other factor. This is as true of the artist as it is of anyone. They are, like everyone else, involved in an inner process that is leading to greater maturity and wisdom. And as they progress on their own inner journey, they are sharing that progress with others. I think we have to trust that they are on their path, and doing what seems best to them. Our challenge is our own inner work, to make sure that we are doing the best that we can do. As I said before, it is easy to point out what other people should be doing more of, but we need to remember that we, too, are "other people" in someone else's eyes.

GROF: I would like to mention in this regard the meetings of the International Transpersonal Association as an example of a situation that provides context for both information and experience. These conferences, held regularly in different parts of the world, bring together people from a variety of disciplines who share the transpersonal orientation or at least interest in the transpersonal field. This includes psychiatrists, psychologists, scientists, educators, clergy, spiritual teachers, economists, and even politicians. The five-day program combines lectures, discussions, rituals, experiential workshops, dancing, and cultural events. These meetings are attended by many artists; as well as getting exposure to a variety of transpersonal ideas from which they can draw inspiration, they also have a unique opportunity to undergo powerful personal experiences. There is no effort to convince or guide anybody—the conferences function by attraction, not by promotion.

LASZLO: In regard to art, too, communication must not be instruction. After all, an artist is a human being who experiences life, and brings a particular sensitivity to this experience. This is bound to reflect in the art that emerges out of his or her esthetic experience.

My point is that if an artist has this sensitivity, then he or she also has a responsibility to make use of it. It is not only his or her own salvation or individual ego that is at stake, but also the well-being of other people and the development of society.

G R O F : Art does not have to carry a direct and explicit message to speak to our time. I am thinking here of the amazing success of the *Star Wars* movies, which did not specifically address the burning issues of our times. It was science fiction with deep archetypal motifs—confrontation of good and evil, a group of people with high ideals defending their freedom against an evil empire, spiritual values versus dehumanized technocratic society, the power of the Force . . . It was happening "once upon a time in a faraway galaxy" and yet it was not difficult to find in it relevance for our present situation.

L A S Z L O : There are a number of examples of this. Another is the series of films launched by *Planet of the Apes*. The public's response to these films was interesting, because in them the human family is confronted as a whole, everyone is in the same situation. All of a sudden our species is dominated by another species, and becomes a kind of slave to it through its own stupidity. Artists could bring this kind of all-human feeling out into the open. Other kinds of science fiction are fascinating as well, but I don't see how they would be directly pertinent to problems on this Earth. There are topics that are far more relevant than interplanetary adventures, and they are not any the less good and interesting for that.

R U S S E L L : The actual story of movies like *Star Wars* may not be relevant to the issues we are currently facing, but the underlying message is very relevant. Along with "May the force be with you" were other very important themes that are universal in their application; things like "anger does not help," and "you must overcome your fears." In most of the successful sci-fi movies you will find similar profound messages that are as applicable and valuable to us today as they are to the characters in their fictional settings. This may be one of the reasons why such movies are successful; they touch a deeper knowing in the soul.

The reason these ideas are creeping into movies is also significant. The people who write and produce the movies are

[vertical right margin: THE SECOND DAY • AFTERNOON]

human beings on their own personal path of self-discovery. When they discover some wisdom in life they naturally want to communicate it to the world. They are asking themselves how they can best put these ideas into a format that gets the message across to as wide an audience as possible. This sort of communication is a subtle process. If you are too preachy people will not listen. The message has to be delivered in the right way, and there is a great skill to that.

But coming back to your question, Ervin, concerning how we already convince artists, I think there are a lot of artists who are convinced.

LASZLO: My question was how we get artists to tune their sensitivity, to extend their antennas, and to become consciously and responsibly relevant to our times.

RUSSELL: But in that question there is the assumption that they are not already doing it.

LASZLO: I am not convinced that all of them are not really doing it—certainly, there are some who are doing it. But I am quite convinced that artists could be doing more than they are doing, and that many more of them could be doing it.

RUSSELL: To me, this sounds like an assumption that somehow we are better than they, that we know more.

LASZLO: That does not necessarily follow. As Bernard Shaw said, to judge an omelette you don't have to know how to lay an egg. We can see the value of artistic production without being able to do it ourselves. We can look at the output of art and say, my goodness, if more of that creativity was focused on the problems we are facing, how much more could it help people see these problems and challenges and be able to respond to them. There is room for improvement here.

G R O F : We are talking about what various groups—scientists, economists, politicians, as well as artists—could or should be doing and how their activities could be catalyzed. I believe that much could be achieved by simply facilitating the exchange of information and encouraging open dialogue within these groups and between them. Another thing that is sorely needed is synthetic, systemic thinking that would bring the mosaic of disconnected new discoveries and insights into a comprehensive whole.

L A S Z L O : Maybe there is such a thing as self-learning—not being taught, but learning by oneself. Couldn't artists come together and deal with the role of art in culture and civilization—their role in the declining phase of Western civilization, as we said, and in the birth of something else in its place. This is an incredible challenge, the greatest challenge artists or anyone else has ever faced.

G R O F : I really believe that a lot could be accomplished by the kind of dialogue that David Bohm recommended. That would include various groups of artists exploring their perspectives on the situation. The artists would become more conscious, more aware of the problems we are facing, and then find their own way of relating to them and expressing them in their art.

R U S S E L L : I think this is a key issue. How can we inspire each other? How can we become catalysts to each other?

G R O F : In my experience, one such powerful catalyst is responsible work with non-ordinary states of consciousness. When I was doing psychedelic research in Czechoslovakia, we had no rigid restrictions on the professional use of these substances. Many of the artists in Prague heard or read about our work and contacted us, asking for psychedelic sessions. We accepted them, since the effect of mind-altering drugs on artistic expression is a very interesting question.

After I emigrated to the US, I could not go back to my native country for over 20 years, because my stay here was considered illegal by the Czech authorities. When I visited Prague after all this time, I had the opportunity to see the exhibitions of a couple of the artists who had psychedelic sessions in our program. The paintings were chronologically arranged and it was immediately obvious when they had the experience. There was a quantum jump in their art. We did not try to change their art; they were fascinated by what we were doing and spontaneously expressed their interest. They used the experience in their own way.

L A S Z L O : We had a similar experience in the Club of Budapest. One of our Creative Members is an English lady, Margaret Smithwhite. She has snow-white hair and beautiful blue eyes, and for the past years has been working with children, getting them to meditate. First she shows them how to enter a meditative state, and then asks them to draw a picture of a peaceful world where children and all people get along together, the kind of world they would like to live in. She works with them for about a week, and gets them to meditate and to draw again and again. At the end of the week one can see an enormous difference in the drawings. We invited her to work for one week at one of the schools in Budapest and then exhibited the children's drawings. The parents came and were amazed. We now have several hundred of these pictures, drawn by children in many parts of the world and from many cultures. Margaret got children of aborigines in Australia, of pre-Columbian Indians in America, of the survival of the disaster in Chernobyl, and of other parts of the world near and far, to meditate and draw pictures. Although each child and each culture had its own vision, they all had certain archetypal elements in common.

And through the experience of meditation there was a tremendous change in what they drew.

Another member of the Club of Budapest, Nato Frascà, is a painter teaching at the Academy of Fine Arts in Rome. For the past 20 years he has been giving an assignment to his students: make some doodles while in a mildly meditative state. Imagine yourself being in the womb, he asks his students, and allow your hand to move over the paper of its own accord. He has collected by now thousands and thousands of these doodles and analyzed them. He developed a system whereby he can make sense of the lines and squiggles. They tell him just when a traumatic event happened in the period of gestation in the womb. (I should add that the traumatic events for the fetus are those periods when it is in danger of being rejected by the mother.) Then, as, Stan, you have found as well, the root of the fear remains in the subconscious of the individual all through his or her life. In Nato's experience it is expressed in the doodles by strong vertical lines. These fall into spaces in the drawings that correspond to given periods of gestation. Nato would analyze the doodles and then ask the student's mother to verify his interpretation: did she really experience something unusual and traumatic at the indicated periods of her pregnancy? It appears that over 90 percent of the time the interpretation is right on the mark.

THE SECOND DAY · AFTERNOON

Values and ethics revisited

L A S Z L O : But let us come back to the question of values. This question has, after all, a major bearing on our lives and our future.

G R O F : Do you mean values that emerge when people have non-ordinary experiences, or values in general?

L A S Z L O : I mean both. But let us first consider the actual nature of values. There has been a tradition, at least in the Western philosophical schools, of regarding values as purely subjective phenomena. But then what follows from this? What is the status of values? They appear to be matters of inscrutable personality factors, mere subjective whims. Yet there is more to values than that. They enter into the world in an objective way: they govern people's behavior. They are also a factor in the interaction between people. Values are both personal and social phenomena, they affect the way communities evolve, and the way they relate to their surroundings. If values are part of the objective world we need to take them seriously, just as seriously as we take health or disease, or any other factor that affects our life and well-being.

GROF: That is certainly true. I believe that there is a system of core values which are transpersonal, which transcend those of the existing cultures. It is an ethical system that emerges spontaneously out of profound mystical experiences. It includes values upon which people from different cultures who have had these experiences would agree. I have seen this phenomenon repeatedly in our work, and the humanistic psychologist Abraham Maslow described it in his observations of people who had spontaneous mystical experiences—or "peak experiences" as he called them. He referred to these values as "metavalues" and the impulses to act according to them as "metamotivations."

LASZLO: When you say transpersonal values, do you mean values that are different from universal or transcultural values?

GROF: That is a good question! It is conceivable that certain values could be transpersonal and yet culture-specific. Maybe "universal" or "transcultural" would be better terms for what I am talking about. They would concern, for example, issues like reverence for life as something that is sacred, the sense that killing is wrong, the sense of compassion for other sentient beings, and so on.

LASZLO: What would be an example of a transpersonal—or universal—value that surfaces in the minds of a great many people?

RUSSELL: I think the one Stan has just mentioned is a good example—the feeling that killing is wrong. We already associate this value with a higher state of consciousness. You would not expect a saint to advocate killing people, indeed you might find it surprising if he advocated killing animals for food. Those who feel it is all right to kill are probably reasoning from an unenlightened state in which the ego-mode of consciousness still rules, the mode that says "My needs come first." Any justification for taking life from another being is nearly always based on some self-centered value system. When people learn to let go of their egocentric mode of being they naturally adopt a greater reverence for life. For them not-killing does not need any rational justification; killing simply feels wrong.

LASZLO: According to mainstream philosophy, moral responsibility is limited to other human beings. We are responsible for our actions *vis-à-vis* others because humans have an "inner" dimension—they suffer if maltreated. On the principle "act toward others as you would wish others to act toward you," philosophers tell us that we must accept responsibility to our fellow human beings. But this limitation of moral responsibility to humans is arbitrary; it is too restrictive. There are good reasons to believe that an inner dimension—a kind of sentience or subjectivity—is shared by all forms of life. And if we believe that, then moral responsibility has to be extended to all forms of life throughout the biosphere.

RUSSELL: Let us just go back a moment and consider the terms we are using. For me, there is a difference between values and morals. Everybody has values. They are "what we value," what we consider important in our lives. These can vary considerably from one person to another, but, as we have just been discussing, we can expect a person's values to change as their mode of consciousness changes. Morals, on the other hand, I think of as the codes laid down by a society as to how a person should behave. They are a set of rules that bind a community together and allow its members to get on with each other.

Many of these morals are attempts to inhibit our self-centeredness, but they do not themselves come from a higher state of consciousness. Most societies have moral injunctions against murder, theft and rape, not necessarily because these are deep values that everybody holds, but because these are principles that society would like its members to uphold. We need these morals in order for a community of egocentric people to function together.

As the consciousness of people rises, there is less need for these morals, less need for society to impose its own set of values. As people go through the kind of experiences Stan has been talking about, they find themselves less bound to the old egocentric modes of consciousness. They are getting more in touch with their own deeper values, and living them more spontaneously. Their values are coming from within rather than from a social code.

LASZLO: There is still a need for a sense of morality. We must still be able to distinguish moral actions from immoral actions.

RUSSELL: I am not sure that this distinction can be made universally. Morals are very relative, and vary from one society to another. What is immoral to one group of people may be perfectly moral to another. Those who are more in touch with themselves and with these deeper universal values are naturally going to act in a way that causes less harm to others. But they may not be acting morally in terms of any specific set of codes. Indeed, they may be behaving immorally as far as some particular society's codes are concerned.

L A S Z L O : Then you say that morality is relative to what is accepted in a given culture.

R U S S E L L : Yes.

G R O F : As long as we remain in the sphere of specific cultures, we find that ethical values are very idiosyncratic, inconsistent, and capricious. What is shocking for one human group can be acceptable and perfectly normal for another. What one society considers to be an absolute and unquestionable imperative, some others do not pay any attention to. And the same applies to various segments of the same culture—social, religious, political, etc.

Let us take as an example sexuality. Once we can free ourselves from the straitjacket of our own cultural bias and see things from a transcultural, universal perspective, we realize how relative and arbitrary are the value judgments in this area. There was a tribe in New Caledonia that used to kill fraternal twins if one was male and the other female, because they violated the incest taboo by sharing the womb. By contrast, in the aristocratic circles in ancient Egypt and Peru, marriage between brother and sister was a sacred duty. Certain cultures have a death penalty for adultery, but an Eskimo custom prescribes the host to offer his wife to a male guest as a compliment of the house. Some cultures consider nudity for both sexes natural and are casual about it, in others women have to cover their entire bodies, including parts of their face. Polygamy, as well as polyandry, is seen as natural and logical by certain cultures. While in some societies homosexuality is considered blasphemy, a crime punishable by death, a form of moral depravity or disease, in others, it is normal and acceptable, or considered even superior to heterosexuality.

But there is also a postconventional morality that transcends the injunctions and prohibitions imposed on us by our culture. That is something altogether different. It is something one feels deeply, almost on a cellular level, something based on a compelling personal experience of a transpersonal nature.

LASZLO: Stan, it seems to me that the remarkable experiences of your patients where they identify even with nonliving things, or with the whole planet or the whole of the cosmos, correlate with a different, non-ordinary value system. Classically, value systems have been pretty egotistic. We have been used to saying, "I don't want to be hurt, therefore I don't hurt others." This is the basis to some extent also of Christian morality, and of any Western morality for that matter. But the Buddhist value system goes beyond it, since all of creation is encompassed in its concerns. Now in the experiences you describe, your subjects go beyond selfish self-interests and value the world at large for what it is. This is, perhaps, because people who undergo these experiences feel that the world is an extension of themselves: they are part of the world, and the world is part of them. So they are moving toward trans-social, even trans-human values, way beyond the kind of values ordinarily associated with morality.

GROF: Yes, you are absolutely right! This becomes evident in systematic spiritual practice that involves deep personal experience. There one can often see continuing ethical development and evolution that happens in stages. Initially, one does not do certain things because of a primitive fear of being caught and punished. On another level, one's actions are guided by a system of commandments or precepts that have become introjected and absorbed into what Freud calls the superego. The next step then is the discovery of the law of karma—one realizes that certain kinds of actions entail certain consequences. The highest form of morality reflects experiential recognition of the unity underlying all of creation, a sense of identity with other sentient beings, and an awareness of our own divinity. In this kind of psychospiritual evolution, the changes of our morality reflect the changes in our understanding of ourselves, of the world, and our place and role in the world.

LASZLO: In your experience, Stan, do people's value horizons become enlarged in the course of such experiences, do they grow and evolve?

GROF: Yes, they do. Certain forms of empathy still involve an element of separation, distinction between me as the observer and the suffering other. There is a difference between ordinary pity, and genuine compassion based on a sense of oneness with others and essential identity with them.

LASZLO: The latter is probably deeper than rational understanding. It appears to be an intuitive sense of one's relationships.

RUSSELL: I agree. Take the example of not causing suffering to others. This idea of harmlessness is something that is found in most spiritual traditions, and is something that many people spontaneously gravitate toward as their consciousness evolves. You know you do not want to suffer yourself, and you do not want to inflict it on others.

This is part of what compassion is about; feeling for other persons as you feel for yourself, and caring for them as you would care for yourself. It is a spontaneous thing that arises as you free your mind from various separating beliefs and attitudes, and begin to feel a deeper empathy with others.

GROF: In non-ordinary states, we can experience conscious identification with anything that is part of existence—people, animals, plants, archetypal beings. For everything that we can perceive normally as an object, there seems to be a corresponding subjective experience. I can feel, for example, that I have become a sequoia tree. My body image takes on the shape of a sequoia, including the roots, the trunk, the branches. I can feel the sap circulating in the cambium, the exchange of minerals and water in the root system, even photosynthesis in the needles. I am not just giving a general example here or describing what happened to somebody I have worked with. I have actually had this experience myself. It was quite extraordinary!

LASZLO: Where do you draw the line when it comes to actually feeling suffering or joy, and the inherent possibility of feeling suffering, joy, and other feelings and emotions? Is the very possibility of feeling and emotion limited to human beings, or does it also apply to other creatures—animals and plants? Or even to the whole of the biosphere . . . ?

RUSSELL: I don't know about plants; they don't seem to have nervous systems like animals do. I don't know whether suffering is dependent upon having a nervous system, and I don't know whether this means they cannot feel pain. But I would certainly take suffering down below vertebrates. I would take it down to insects. I would not be happy pulling the legs off a spider, because I imagine that the spider feels pain.

LASZLO: I wonder if the connections between the leaves and branches of a tree and its trunk wouldn't qualify for registering pain of some sort. Would pulling off leaves or branches produce a qualitative kind of sensation in the plant?

RUSSELL: I really don't know; I can look only at my own experience. To me it feels wrong to pull the legs off a spider, but I can go and pick a leaf off a tree without feeling any great anguish. So I suppose I have drawn a mental line somewhere between a spider and a tree.

LASZLO: Well, I am not sure I would. I am inclined to think that when a hydrogen atom is bombarded by radiation even it "feels" something qualitative that is analogous to the most basic forms of pain.

GROF: There seems to be an infinite variety of discomfort associated with processes on all levels of existence. We talked earlier about Whitehead. One reason why I think that he did not really adequately cover the full range of what one experiences in transpersonal states is that he sees consciousness as the very last stage of the process of concrescence.

RUSSELL: Yes, but didn't Whitehead believe that interiority, not necessarily consciousness as we know it, but an inner world of some kind, went all the way down the evolutionary tree, right down to the basic elements of matter?

LASZLO: In his view there are "societies of actual entities" which have their own interiority, and these include even molecules.

GROF: He also wrote that each actual entity contains the entire history of the universe up to that moment. Normally, we are not consciously aware of all that constitutes the present moment, of everything that flows into it. We could use his model, but we would need to assume that in non-ordinary states certain specific aspects of that history suddenly emerge into awareness and become fully conscious. It could involve people, animals, plants, inorganic objects, and even archetypes or, in Whitehead's terminology, "eternal objects."

LASZLO: Given such a broad range of identifications one's value system is bound to become less egocentric, less limited. This kind of altered state identification could be a powerful socializing factor in the world.

GROF: It could indeed.

Ultimate Questions: Some Concluding Reflections

Karma

LASZLO: We have touched on a number of basic, perhaps even ultimate, questions. Perhaps we should look at some of them again. What can we learn from them? Take, for example, the remarkable powers and faculties that seem to emerge when people enter altered states of consciousness.

GROF: When people get involved in self-exploration using non-ordinary states of consciousness, it is not necessary to teach them ecology or ethics. When they have transpersonal experiences, their system of values changes automatically and they develop deep ecological awareness, tolerance, and compassion. Experiences of psychospiritual death and rebirth have a similar effect; one's sense of identity is expanded and includes other beings. The experience of ego-death leads to the sense of a much larger identity.

This process has very important practical consequences. We had a program of psychedelic therapy for terminal cancer patients facing imminent death. These kind of experiences helped them overcome the fear of death and changed profoundly their attitude, the quality of their remaining days, and the experience of dying.

RUSSELL: I spoke earlier of my friend who died recently. Something interesting happened to her in her last days; she became at peace with her own death. For a whole year she had been really fighting death. I remember her saying, I'm not ready to go yet, I don't want to go yet, I'm not ready to go. Then, a week or two before she died, she was saying, Do you think I should go yet? Or should I hang around a bit longer? She was very relaxed about it, all fear seemed to have gone. It was quite amazing.

I sometimes think we should all go through this early in our lives. Not the actual dying, of course, but the letting go of the fear of dying. Ideally this should be part of our education; we should be helped to move beyond this fear so that we can live the rest of our adult lives without this huge invisible weight hanging around our necks. It would be a very, very different world.

GROF: I understand that the ancient mysteries of death and rebirth, and also the rites of passage of the native cultures, enabled people to go through a kind of dying before dying. The 17th-century German Augustinian monk Abraham of Santa Clara put it very succinctly: The man who dies before he dies does not die when he dies. Once you have this experience, you do not see death as the end of who you are, but as a fantastic journey, as a transition to a different mode and level of existence. Whether this is a profound cosmic truth or a merciful delusion, as some of the materialistic critics of transpersonal psychology assert, it can certainly transform people's lives.

LASZLO: Some intuitions about death and rebirth are thousands of years old and still unmatched in their profundity. What is so beautiful about the *Tibetan Book of the Dead*, for example, is the guidance it provides for the spirit or soul after death. What is very difficult to accept of that guidance, on the other hand, is that rebirth is not a liberation but a kind of bondage. Up to the very last moment the spirit of the dead is fighting for liberation into nirvana, against being reborn. The last stage of the fight is how to close the entrance to the womb of the mother to whom one would be otherwise reborn. Whereas in our value system the best thing would be to be reborn, in good circumstances of health and wealth.

G R O F : There are different opinions about this in various spiritual systems and in Buddhism itself. Certainly the original Hinayana Buddhists did not see much value in incarnated existence. The material realm was for them a quagmire of death and rebirth, the domain of suffering. The solution they offered was to extinguish the "thirst of flesh and blood," extricate oneself from incarnate existence and reach nirvana. The term "nirvana" has the same root as wind (*vatah*) and means literally evanescence. But the later Mahayana Buddhism teaches that we can attain nirvana in the world by eliminating the three "poisons" from our life: ignorance, desire, and aggression.

Some spiritual systems see the goal as attaining union with God, with the undifferentiated divine. I have discussed this issue in my last book, *The Cosmic Game*, which describes the philosophical and metaphysical insights from non-ordinary states. There is a big problem with defining the spiritual goal this way. People who actually have the experience of union with the divine realize that this principle is not only the goal and final destination of the spiritual journey, but also the source of creation. If this state were so self-fulfilling and complete in its pristine undifferentiated form, creation would not have happened. Creating phenomenal worlds of separation is thus a necessary aspect of God, and the world we live in has something important to offer.

There does not seem to be a solution or satisfying answer on either end. The undifferentiated divine needs to create, and the units of consciousness split off in the world of plurality crave to return back to the original unity. So the question arises: is it possible to find an intelligent adaptation to this dynamic tension in the cosmic system, and if so, what is it? Clearly, the solution is not to reject embodied existence as inferior and worthless and try to escape from it. Any satisfactory solution will have to embrace both the earthly and the transcendental dimensions, both the world of forms and the formless.

The material universe as we know it offers countless possibilities for extraordinary adventures in consciousness. Only in the physical form and on the material plane can we fall in love, enjoy the ecstasy of sex, have children, listen to Beethoven's music, or admire Rembrandt's paintings. Only on Earth can we listen to the song of a nightingale or taste bouillabaisse and baked alaska. However, when our identification with the body-ego is absolute and our belief in the material world the only reality, it is impossible to fully enjoy our participation in creation. We are haunted by the awareness of our personal insignificance, the impermanence of everything, and the inevitable nature of death.

To find the solution to this dilemma, we have to turn inward. When we have sufficient experiential knowledge of the transpersonal aspects of existence, including our own true identity and cosmic status, everyday life becomes much easier and more rewarding. As our inner search continues, we sooner or later discover the essential emptiness behind all forms. As the Buddhist teachings suggest, knowledge of the virtual nature of the phenomenal world and its voidness can help us achieve freedom from suffering. This includes the recognition that belief in separate selves in our life, including our own, is ultimately an illusion.

L ASZLO : The whole idea of karma is meaningful and captivating—the idea that there is an ongoing process of growth and development throughout life, and then through and across death. You can improve your state in each lifetime until you reach a higher dimension. That is a very meaningful view of life—and of death.

G ROF : Many years ago, I was invited to a conference in Washington convened by US senator Claiborne Pell. Its theme was the possibility of survival of consciousness after death. It featured people with impressive academic credentials and some prominent spiritual teachers; we addressed this topic with all seriousness and academic rigor. Rupert Sheldrake's talk was on the possibility of our memories surviving death, Charles Tart examined the relevant material from parapsychological research, and I discussed the observations from consciousness research supporting the possibility of survival. Tibetan lama Sogyal Rinpoche and archbishop John Sponge brought their respective religious perspectives to the discussion.

The resulting impression from all these presentations was that there exists enough evidence to take the problem seriously and subject it to systematic research. For example, Ian Stevenson's meticulous studies of children remembering previous incarnations are impressive. The Tibetan anecdotal accounts of the tests to which they subject the children whom they suspect to be specific incarnated lamas are also fascinating. So are the observations on veridical out-of-body experiences in near-death situations.

L ASZLO: I had an interesting exchange of ideas with Ian Stevenson on the interpretation of reincarnation phenomena. I do not believe that it is necessary to interpret the phenomena—the recall of what appear to be memories from other lifetimes—as evidence for the reincarnation of a soul. One can also interpret the recollections that surface from apparent previous lifetimes as paranormal access to transpersonal information, that is, as information that comes to us from the minds and experiences of other people, and only appears to be memories—rather strange memories—of our own.

G ROF: In any event, the problems of the survival of consciousness and of reincarnation are not just issues of theoretical interest, but have serious practical consequences. How we answer the question of survival for ourselves has profound impact on our behavior. In the global crisis that we are facing, this could make much difference. The one-timer view of life tells us that if we can avoid secular justice and retaliation for our sins and mistakes, there is no further responsibility we need to take for them.

L ASZLO: People fight for all the privileges and pleasures they get in their one, supposedly unique, lifetime. As a popular ad for beer said, "you only go around once in life." This is reinforcing consumerism and hedonism. You want to get the best you can in this life, because that is all there is to life.

G ROF: Our beliefs concerning reincarnation also have serious moral implications. As Plato said: to believe that there is nothing beyond death would be a "boon for the wicked."

R USSELL: On the other hand societies that believe in some form of survival may use that as a form of control or manipulation. If you don't behave yourself now, and live what we consider to be a righteous life and follow our particular set of codes, then you will be punished afterwards.

G ROF: But the concept of karma does not imply retaliation or punishment. It is a cosmic law describing the automatic consequences of our actions. We can get to know this law, understand it, and use this knowledge as a guiding principle for our behavior. It is more like knowing that fire by its nature will burn us if we come too close, or that objects will fall if we stop supporting them. When we act in an ignorant way and treat others as fundamentally different and separate from us, we sink deeper into the world of matter, illusion, and suffering. To the extent that we treat them as if they were ourselves, to that extent we move toward the world of oneness and spirit.

R USSELL: The idea of karma as we think of it today may not be the same as in its original meaning. Initially it probably came from a very simple insight which, like many other spiritual ideas, was modified and embellished as it was passed down over the years. The Sanskrit word *karma* literally means "action," and may initially have referred to the simple but profoundly important realization that we are bound to action and its effects. We do not act in empty space; our actions inevitably create ripples in our environment, and we partake in the effects of those ripples as much as anyone else. As Christianity puts it, "as you sow, so shall you reap." This does not have to imply any cosmic accounting system, whereby you get back exactly what you put out, only a general principle that we cannot avoid.

L A S Z L O : Part of the original view was the cycle of reincarnations. So whatever you do now in this lifetime, is only part of your existence, for your existence is ongoing.

G R O F : In my work with non-ordinary states of consciousness I have often seen a typical progression in people from our culture in regard to the problem of reincarnation. An average Westerner comes into this work with a one-timer view. He or she considers the idea of reincarnation to be nonsense. It seems absolutely obvious that our lifespan is limited to the period from conception to biological death. We are our bodies, and consciousness is a product of our brains. When our physical bodies perish, that is the absolute and irrevocable end of who we are, including our consciousness.

The experiences of past-life memories are so compelling and convincing, however, that they usually change this attitude dramatically. We experience something from another century and/ or country and have a sense of authentic recall of these events (*déjà vu, déjà vecu*). In this process we can not only understand some of our emotional and psychosomatic problems as carryovers from the past situation, we can also free ourselves from them when the experience is completed. These experiences can provide access to extraordinary new information about other historical periods and cultures.

In view of all these facts, the individual who is undergoing transpersonal experiences has good reason to take reincarnation seriously, and even to get preoccupied with it as something more important than the events of this life. It is known that traumatic events in infancy and childhood can deeply distort and contaminate our later life; this is what much of conventional psychotherapy is about. Suddenly, a traumatic pattern is found, however, that seems to be contaminating not just one lifetime, but an entire chain of consecutive incarnations, one after the other. Once people realize that, they may turn into "karma hunters."

So what is happening here? People who previously saw themselves as temporarily and spatially limited, as "one-timer body-egos," transcend in their experience the limitations of linear time. These experiences convince them that they have lived before, and very likely will reincarnate again in the future. However, to hold this belief they have to remain convinced that they are spatially separated from others. Without separate protagonists there could not be any karma.

As their search continues, people can have yet other types of experiences which convince them that their sense of separate identity is an illusion, that they are part of a unified field of cosmic consciousness which includes everything and everybody else. Then they stop believing in karma, because they see even the karmic stories as a product of maya, the cosmic illusion. But the new disbelief in karma is significantly different from the original skepsis. Because now they know that one can be in a state of consciousness where the idea of reincarnation appears absurd. They realize that certain kinds of experiences might convince one that karma is all-important. And they can experience transcending even that stage. There is no single unambiguous answer to the question of karma. It all depends on the evolutionary stage of consciousness one is in.

L a s z l o : It appears that there may be various karmas possible in the higher phase, accessed according to the level one has achieved in one's lifetime. In a sense, one can have an influence on the choice of one's next lifetime.

GROF: In the Tibetan Vajrayana there are stories about high lamas who are able to maintain full consciousness during their passage through all three bardos, the intermediate states that one experiences between death and next incarnation. Others are allegedly able to predict or even determine when, where, and as who they are going to be incarnated in their next lifetime.

I would like to mention something that I did not sufficiently emphasize when we talked about reincarnation. An essential characteristic of a past life experience is an authentic sense of recall: This is not the first time this is happening to me. I remember that I once actually was that person. There are other experiences that can take us to other times and other places. We can also experience something taking place at another time of human history and at another place, but without the element of personal memories. For example, we may experience ourselves as an Inca priest, a Roman soldier, or a drunken Mexican woman, but without the sense of personal relation to that experience. It is simply a kind of window into the Jungian collective unconscious.

Modern physics has demonstrated that there are no separate objects in the world and that the universe is a unified web of subatomic processes. And yet, in our everyday life, we have a special proprietary sense about our individual lives, our bodies, and our egos. When the process of self-exploration reaches the collective unconscious, all the human lives throughout history are our lives. As I mentioned earlier, in the last analysis, they all have only one protagonist, Absolute Consciousness, Brahman, the Tao, or whatever term we use for it. But we have a special proprietary feeling about some of these lives and experience them as *"our* past lives." We have not let go of our ego, we hold onto the remnants of our separate identity.

LASZLO: Do you see past-life experiences as evidence that there is an integrated bundle of consciousness that survives physical death and gets reincarnated, for that would appear to be a relatively simplistic concept?

GROF: No, not necessarily. For example, for the Hindus, the doctrine of reincarnation is not a belief in the usual sense—an unsubstantiated and ungrounded opinion—but an eminently pragmatic issue. It is an attempt to provide a conceptual framework for a large number of extraordinary experiences and observations. But even in the Hindu tradition the belief in the continuity of the same separate unit of consciousness that repeatedly reincarnates over many consecutive lifetimes would be considered a low-level, primitive interpretation of the facts.

According to more sophisticated Hindu teachings, there is only one being that actually incarnates, and that is Brahman. As long as one has more than one protagonist in one's story, one is still under the influence of the cosmic illusion, or maya. Existence is a unified field and any boundaries that we experience within it are ultimately relative and can be transcended. We can experience ourselves as a separate body-ego, we can experience identification with all the mothers of the world, or humanity as a whole, or the entire biosphere. But ultimately all these boundaries are arbitrary and negotiable.

Consciousness

LASZLO: The way people in modern societies have experienced themselves—the notion they have had of the human being himself or herself—has changed a great deal, even in this century. Yet the public image of the human being is still not up to where it would be if it were adequate for living on this small and interdependent planet. Just what is the image of the human being today, and in particular, what is the view regarding the nature of his or her consciousness? The way these questions are answered may be decisive of the way people behave in concrete circumstances.

RUSSELL: The image of who we are is changing already. The old model is that human beings are somehow different from other creatures, that we are special because we have consciousness and other creatures do not. This view is not only part of the scientific mainstream, but also part of classical Christianity. And it raises various difficult questions. What is it about human beings that makes them conscious? How does consciousness arise from inanimate matter? The new view which is gaining increasing respect is that the difference between us and other creatures is not consciousness as such, but difference in the *degree* of consciousness.

Consider dogs, for example. Dogs seem to feel pain—if we did not believe they feel pain, we would not give them anesthetics when we operated on them. Dogs also appear to dream when they are asleep, they recognize people and places, and they can act with a purpose in mind. To say a dog is not conscious, that it has no internal world of experience is as ridiculous as saying that my neighbor across the street is not conscious. Where we differ from dogs is not in consciousness itself, but in what goes on in our consciousness. We humans can think in words, can reason, can understand the world in which we live, can think about the future and make decisions, and are aware of our own selves and the fact that we are conscious.

What applies to dogs also applies to other mammals; cats, horses, dolphins—they all have an inner experience of the world. So, I imagine, do birds, snakes, frogs and fishes. They are all vertebrates with a brain, spinal chord and sensory organs similar in basic design to ours. The question is not why are human beings conscious, but how far down the evolutionary tree does consciousness go?

I find it difficult to draw a line anywhere. Insects have simple nervous systems, why shouldn't they be conscious, even if it be a tiny fraction of our consciousness? Maybe nervous systems are not the originators of consciousness, but just the amplifiers of consciousness. Perhaps single cells have a rudimentary form of consciousness. It may be virtually nothing compared with the richness of experience that we know, but who is to say they have absolutely no experience whatsoever?

From this perspective it is not consciousness itself that has evolved; the faculty of consciousness is part of life. What has evolved as life has evolved is, as I said, the degree of consciousness.

LASZLO: This is just what I had in mind when we talked about feeling pain and joy in the context of ethics and morality. I strongly suspect that even molecules and atoms have some form of interiority, some element resembling a subjective sensation. This notion, of course, is not new: it is familiar from the history of philosophy both in the East and in the West.

But could you elaborate further on the notion of a universal consciousness that gets specified as regards its degree of explicitness in the course of evolution?

RUSSELL: To understand the universal nature of consciousness a useful analogy is a picture painted on a canvas. The picture that is painted depends upon the colors available, the quality of the brushes, the inspiration of the artist, but whatever picture is painted, however simple or complex it may be, the canvas is the same and it is absolutely necessary. Without the canvas there would be no picture. In the same way, the faculty of consciousness is an absolute prerequisite for any experience. What varies are the images that appear in consciousness. The simplest creatures experience the simplest of pictures of reality. Creatures with evolved sense organs can experience more detail in the world around, painting a correspondingly richer image of the world in their mind. More complex nervous systems have led to deeper processing of the sensory data, and a more integrated picture of reality.

The principal reason human consciousness is so much richer than the consciousness of other animals stems from the fact that we have evolved the capacity for speech. We can communicate to each other in words, which are essentially symbols denoting various aspects of our experience. This means that we can share our experiences with each other. A dog learns primarily from its own experience of the world, and has to build up its knowledge from scratch. Human beings learn not only from their experience, but also from the experience of others. As a result we have built up a collective body of knowledge far greater than any one individual could ever attain. This is why we have education; we want to impart our understandings to others so they can benefit from what others have learnt.

But perhaps the most significant addition to come from language is the ability to think. We not only use words to communicate with each other, we also internalize language, we think in words within our own minds. From this has come the ability to reason, to think about the past, to imagine the future, to make choices, to think about our experiences. From this also has come self-consciousness; we are aware that we are aware. We are conscious that we are conscious.

LASZLO: The faculty of being conscious of being conscious—what is called "reflexive consciousness"—opens up a whole new dimension of experience to those who possess it.

RUSSELL: The self-reflective nature of our consciousness opens us up to the divine. The capacity for sentience of one form or another, which is common to all sentient beings, is close to mystical notions of God. Mystics throughout history, and from a diversity of cultures, have repeatedly claimed a personal identity of the self and God. In Hindu philosophy we find it in the statement that Atman, the essence of our consciousness, is Brahman, the essence and source of all existence. In Christian traditions this insight may have been voiced as the claim that "I am God"—although this has landed many mystics into trouble with the Church, for such statements are considered heresy.

At present science does not pay much attention to this universal nature of consciousness. It is still caught in the old model which says that space, time and matter are the primary reality, that consciousness somehow emerges from them. But as science begins to take the subject of consciousness more seriously, it is going to have to develop a new paradigm in which consciousness is seen to be as primary as space, time, and matter. And from there it will find that it has opened up to a whole new understanding of what religion has been pointing toward for thousands of years. Not the classical "old man in the sky" sort of God, but a notion of God that ties in perfectly with our scientific understanding of the world. That is when the really interesting shift will begin to happen. It is not happening yet, but I believe that we are moving toward it.

G ROF : Many hard-core representatives of mainstream materialistic science would violently disagree with some of the things you are saying, Pete, for example, that the capacity to be conscious runs through all of life or all of creation, and that our deepest essence is divine. I remember some of the extreme statements that were made after Norbert Wiener formulated the basic principles of cybernetics. For example, it became possible to construct mechanical foxes capable of pursuing a rabbit without having any subjective notion of its existence. It was seriously suggested that all animals are like that—nothing but mechanical systems lacking any subjective awareness and propelled by complex sequences of stimulus and response. It was, of course, difficult to deny consciousness to humans, since we all experience it.

Yet what you are saying is not just a vague metaphysical assumption or pseudo-philosophical speculation. What materialistic critics fail to take into consideration is the fact that we have vast experiential evidence supporting these claims. As I said earlier, in non-ordinary states it is very common to experience conscious identification with other life forms, including viruses and plants, and even various inorganic aspects of the cosmos. It could be argued that this is not a direct proof that everything around us is conscious. But, at the very least, transpersonal experiences suggest that such a possibility is very real. Similarly, the fact that we can experience our identity with the divine is undeniable and has been repeatedly confirmed by modern consciousness research.

I cannot imagine a convincing theory that would offer a sober materialistic explanation for the existence, nature, and content of all these experiences. So the critical question is what you have raised, Ervin, during the past two days—the origins and reality status of these experiences. Do they reveal some profound truth about the nature of reality, or are they fantasies and hallucinations? Forty years of studying these fascinating phenomena have convinced me that they have to be taken seriously.

Traditional academic science describes human beings as highly developed animals and biological thinking machines. Experiences and observations in the everyday state of consciousness strongly suggest that we are Newtonian objects made of atoms, molecules, cells, tissues, and organs. However, transpersonal experiences clearly show that each of us can also manifest the properties of an infinite field of consciousness that transcends space, time, and linear causality. The complete new formula, remotely reminiscent of the wave–particle paradox in modern physics, would describe humans as paradoxical beings who have two complementary aspects: they can show properties of Newtonian objects, and also those of infinite fields of consciousness. The appropriateness of each of these descriptions depends on the state of consciousness in which the observations are made.

LASZLO: It is curious that in the last few years the term "consciousness" has come to be used for what used to be called "mind," or just the sensitivity or subjectivity associated with living organisms. Consciousness, in much of the earlier literature, was reserved to what one can properly view as the uniquely human faculty of self-awareness. If you are conscious, you are conscious of your own thoughts and sensations. In this context we can talk about something that is specifically human, because the seat of self-reflexive consciousness seems to be located in the neocortex, and the neocortex is only developed to a corresponding extent in the human species—though higher primates seem to be on an evolutionary path toward it. Subjectivity, however, which is not the same as reflexive consciousness, is just the faculty of having sensations, and I believe that this is associated with every system that exists and evolves in nature.

As Pete just pointed out, there is no reasonable cut-off point in our attribution of subjectivity in nature. If you say your dog has subjectivity, then you must say that also the mouse has it, and so on down the line. The simplest living organisms must be seen as having subjectivity, and if so, then why not also their components, the macromolecules, molecules, and atoms? The seeds of consciousness must be present in the universe—they must be everywhere.

R USSELL: Yes, consciousness is as fundamental to the universe as matter, space and time—absolutely fundamental.

L ASZLO: Consciousness becomes more and more specified in the course of time and evolution. It is a remarkable achievement of our species that our brain and body develop the seeds of consciousness that are ubiquitous in nature into the capacity for self-reflection. This is like adding a monitor that is not keyed to mapping the world beyond the body, but is keyed to mapping the mapping of the world.

R USSELL: That is what makes human beings special, the fact that we have this self-reflective consciousness. I don't think other creatures have this ability. At least other creatures like dogs and cats that do not think to themselves as we do. Dolphins and whales may, but we have very little idea at the moment of what goes on in their minds.

L ASZLO: I agree. That is why we have a personal identity, because once we have self-awareness, we are able to see ourselves as part of the world. Of course, we can also make mistakes and see ourselves as being opposed to the world, or being separate from it. We can say, this is me, and this is my skin that encloses it. Everything else is not me. We can look at everything that is not-me as radically different from what is me. Then we get bogged down in the egocentric predicament and in all the limitations and restrictions that follow from it. Can we in the last count really know anything other than our own mind and consciousness? In the materialistic view, the self-reflective ego becomes radically separate from the world.

G ROF: Yet people who get involved in systematic deep self-exploration using non-ordinary states of consciousness, such as meditation, experiential psychotherapy, or responsible use of psychedelics, tend to develop a distinct and unified view or vision of themselves and reality. The same is true for those who have powerful spontaneous experiences of this kind—spiritual emergencies or near-death experiences. The basic characteristics of this new attitude toward life are a sense of deep connection with other people, other species and nature, concern about the planetary future, and spirituality of a universal and all-encompassing nature. Additional important considerations are a reorientation toward renewable sources of energy, the need to clean the environment, and a tendency to return to natural cycles. In other words, orientation toward activities that are critical for a sustainable future.

R USSELL: Language and thinking may have given us a sense of self, but most of us are only half-awake and half-aware of who we really are. And this, too, has its handicaps. As we discussed earlier, we tend to derive our sense of identity from what we do, what we have, how others perceive us, and our role in the world. Such an identity is very fragile and continually at the mercy of circumstances. Trying to maintain and bolster this derived sense of identity leads us into all manner of inappropriate and damaging behaviors. Spiritual traditions the world over are aligned in their admonition that we need to awaken to a deeper sense of self, and discover who we really are. Then we discover true freedom.

From this perspective spiritual practice can be thought of as ways to overcome some of the handicaps of language so that we can go on to realize our true potential as sentient beings.

G ROF: What you are saying, Pete, brings back a memory of a discussion I had many years ago with a man who was coming down from a psychedelic session in which he had to take a deep look at the meaning of his life. He had realized in the course of this experience that much of what he was doing with his life was inauthentic and unsatisfying; his heart was not really in it. Much of it was driven by unfulfilled dreams and expectations of his parents, and by an effort to prove something to them and to himself. He also discovered how strong were the programs inculcated in him by his culture, and how much of his behavior was shaped by peer pressure and external circumstances.

At one point, he said to me: You know, I think that the most important task in our life is to find out what is our "nasturtium consciousness." I did not, of course, know the term since he just had made it up, and I asked him for clarification. Well, it does not have to be nasturtium. It can be any other flower or plant, he answered. Just look at them! They all are in immediate contact with the Earth, with the Sun and with the rain, and just do their thing. A nasturtium does not aspire to be a rose. It is not concerned whether it ends up in a wedding bouquet, in a bowl of salad, eaten by a rabbit, or stepped on by a cow. And then he went on to tell me that he felt that behind all the inauthentic programs imposed on us by the circumstances of our life, lies a germane specific cosmic script for each of us. That for him was nasturtium consciousness. When we discover what it is and use it as our guiding principle, our life becomes creative, fulfilling, and easy. Joseph Campbell referred to this as "following your bliss."

LASZLO: As soon as we have a reflective consciousness we have the capacity to give meaning to experience, and it does not have to be a materialistic Western common-sense meaning. When a living being does not have this consciousness, it just experiences: the experience is its own meaning. I would think that a dog or another animal perceives things directly and does not reflect on them. This has some major consequences. If an animal makes mistakes, they get corrected by natural selection. For example, if rabbits regularly mistook a snake for a stick, that line of rabbits would become extinct very fast. But we humans continually make mistakes in our view of ourselves and our environment and we compensate for them. Such compensation does not make a mistaken view into a correct one, but it makes it more difficult to recognize the mistaken view. In consequence we can have a number of different views of ourselves and the world, and some of them will be more functional in regard to our survival than others.

Beyond functionality, of course, there is the philosophical or metaphysical question as to what is ultimately true. Being able to pose this question but not answer it with final certainty is the human predicament. For we cannot see the world except through our own perceptions and interpretations—we have access only to our mappings, and not to pristine reality. But, evidently, some worldviews and conceptions are not only more conducive to survival and development than others, they are also more likely to be true. It is in our own interest to move toward these "better" interpretations. They give us the most consistent and penetrating answers to the ultimate questions we all ask sooner or later.

At the same time, we have found that the emerging consciousness is a true evolutionary step—one that brings us closer to the fundamental truths about ourselves and the world; truths that are part of the cultural heritage of contemporary people, yet were ignored or repressed in the heady progress of materialistic science and its technological civilization. Now, as science as well as society confronts the challenge of a further evolutionary leap, the perspectives that open for us include the discovery, and the re-discovery, of deeper insights about life, cosmos, and consciousness. These are exciting times to be alive—and to dialogue, and to act.

It is late, and the time has come to close this dialogue and take our leave. We have had two full and exciting days, with discussions that covered a whole gamut of issues, from our personal development to the evolution of all of humanity. We began with questions concerning the chances of peace in the world, and returned time and time again to the notion that the evolution of our consciousness is the key—the key to peace in the world, as well as to our personal and collective survival and development. While the problems we have noted are serious and challenging, we did not settle for passive pessimism. We found a silver lining on the horizon: the changes that are actually occurring in people's values, thinking, worldviews—in their consciousness. This we called the 'consciousness revolution," a phenomenon we have rightly regarded as a positive sign of our times—a sign that humankind, a cultural as well as biological species, is responding to the threats and challenges it faces in these crucial yet fascinating times.

THE SECOND DAY · EVENING

Afterword—Further Reflections

When Ervin Laszlo kindly asked me to contribute some further reflections to this stimulating book, I found myself writing a personal commentary which took me back to my childhood. *The Consciousness Revolution* is a record of meetings in Sausalito and San Francisco between Ervin Laszlo, Peter Russell, and Stanislav Grof. I remember that Sausalito was at the end of the ferry shuttle from Market Street in San Francisco, where at weekends the queue extended for miles and we had to wait hours to board the ferry. In those relatively innocent days, tens of thousands of San Franciscans set out from here with knapsacks to explore Muir Woods and Mount Tamalpais. An amusing locomotive with vertical pistons pulled a little train of open cars and on the way down they were allowed to glide, pulled by gravity. Recalling such memories brought back to me issues which have preoccupied me all my life and which were reawakened on reading *The Consciousness Revolution*.

I believe we have actually *become unconscious*. To alter this state of mind, it is not simply a matter of setting out to acquire new dimensions of consciousness. What is required of us is a return from the self-conscious protective armor we have built around us to an almost unconscious state which explores our own inbuilt affinity with the All, of which we are a part.

In order to prevent what many of us now feel is almost inevitable collective suicide, we must learn how to allow the potential which exists in all of us to manifest itself. At birth we bring to our lives memories of our species, genetic structure, a universal awareness of infinity, and the ability to listen to ourselves. We learn to use our senses to hear and see, giving us the ability to appreciate and create art and music; we develop intellectually, acquiring knowledge and skills, and we progress through life expressing ourselves to the best of our abilities. Yet we do not understand how to express our sense of the infinite within us. We try to turn it into something impossibly tangible, substantial and powerful in order to have total control of ourselves and our world. It seems that the only way to convey our sense of eternity without corrupting our ambitions is through artistic and creative expression, through the creation of a work which can be infinitely beautiful—an example of how creativity can redeem the crude and gross aspects of life. I would say that without art and without humility our sense of infinity has little opportunity of expression other than in continual demands for infinite power to own, to dominate, and to exercise total control. When the ego is in control, our hunger for power has no limits. The individual can be seen as only "a cog in the machine" but, beyond the ego, we all have a self with knowledge of the secret of living cells and a belief in the possibility of a mystical union with the All.

Even if this belief is unconscious, we all crave a return to divine experience. To return to divinity involves a certain sacrifice. Acts of self-sacrifice to appease the gods have been a feature of many more "primitive" societies than ours. Our God today is Mammon—money and commerce—and our sacrifice is global. Nationalist feeling, for example, encourages people to believe that it is their duty to sacrifice themselves and others, to protect sacred symbols and principles, thus giving nationalism holy significance. Women and children are still the chief sacrifice, perhaps in a less ritualistic manner than before but still on an appalling scale. In some places Muslim children believe that death is the highest reward and rush (or are driven) to their death in hundreds of thousands, mobilized to become excellent, reliable killers. So we have inherent in us a call of the divine, obedience, ideals, but all organized in the service of a conscious Devil. We are aware of the principle of universal unity but we use it for the most hideous purposes and to the most ignorant, narrowing, and suicidal ends.

Our systems of justice, based on punishment instead of on

the protection of victims and the rehabilitation and redemption of offenders, are totally wrong. Punishment offers little chance of education or improvement. Laws imposing arbitrarily different degrees of punishment are next to useless, as are the armies of lawyers analyzing indecipherable legal texts and juries humanly *un*qualified to judge each case on its own merits or demerits. Since Nuremberg there have been attempts to create a World Court but it is only by prevention that we can save lives and improve our prospects of protecting world civilizations and cultures.

Our natural resources are sufficient to sustain populations only up to a certain level. Even in a more inclusive democracy with representation for the oppressed, weak, sick, less educated, vulnerable and differently able, we would be unable to prevent the stronger and more ruthless from seizing food, land, water, and other resources. In humanitarian terms we have vast resources of compassion, guilt, obligation, moral codes, and religion. Money is in a real way democratic power, for a dollar remains a dollar no matter what the color or the condition of the hand that holds it, yet such is the abuse of money it can buy whole nations and it is now essential to establish money-free zones which promote active and direct relationships independently.

The persuasive powers of advertising, of political propaganda and of religions, are very similar. Their methods are identical, manipulative and misleading and for the most part consist of unfulfillable promises: for example, China and the USA are both pursuing the accumulation of power to exploit and control the abuse of natural and human resources. Under pressure of unrelenting circumstances, this situation could turn into war. If our worst inclination can be justified theoretically or blessed by an ideal, and if we are left with no choice but to fulfill it, we stand alone before our conscience.

Both despite and because of the huge advances in medicine, psychology, agriculture, nutrition, technology, communications, and leisure facilities, human beings have been reduced to a "battery" existence, and soon we may witness the wholesale decimation of our species on a scale reminiscent of the pandemic plagues of the past, occurring simultaneously from numerous causes and sources. In fact, it has begun already—bankruptcy, unemployment, disease, famine, social chaos exist now in the USA as well as in less wealthy nations, and a new order of values is necessary if we are to survive at a personal and global level.

The problem is this: can we choose the most humane way to learn the lesson we need to learn without causing such negative consequences as radiation, revenge, devastation, or psychological damage? Can we make "the world safe" for goodness as well as "for democracy" (to paraphrase Woodrow Wilson)? Good values are those that affect the greatest number positively—encouragement, understanding, patience, quiet courage—involving the greatest trust and the least corrosion and wear. Artists, dreamers, and inventors play an essential role in combating prejudice and violence, especially in conveying ideas and values to children; for example, my MUS-E project which brings music and arts to European schools has shown how a very basic innovation can help change consciousness.

The most difficult concepts a human being can learn are moderation, a sense of proportion and a knowledge of limitations. The difficulty is in expanding time and space to focus outward from the hunt of our prey toward the protection of our victim, from the here and now to the wider dimensions where compassion stands in the way of greed. Can we adopt a system of education which will help us to be kind and courageous, forgiving and determined, trusting but realistic, wise and generous rather than clever and selfish? Can we allow our daily actions and behavior to be guided by creative, artistic, esthetic principles? Can we desist from imbuing our children with prejudice and fear? Can we remove violence and brutality from our screens, books, thoughts, ambitions, or is this our way of preparing ourselves for the catastrophes which await us?

I believe in the unity of "inner" and "outer." The great German philosopher Constantin Brunner said that everything is conscious in degree—and we know scientifically that radiation can penetrate light years, so could we likewise be penetrated by "consciousness," like a vibrating neutron? Perhaps this is how we can bring about a revolution in consciousness, by generating and encouraging new attitudes and beliefs which will permeate our thoughts, our actions, and our institutions, from medicine, psychology, and philosophy to science, commerce, banking, religion, and the arts. Our lives are meant to be lived in full awareness of other people, of animals, of the potential of our minds—the beauty of art, and the joy of true communication which gives equal importance to the time and place of the message, the messenger, and the person receiving the message. This is how creation is diffused, in different situations and conditions, and one of the results is that the idea of originality is diluted; we can see how certain ideas and inventions occur simultaneously in places far removed from each other. I have been amazed how often "like draws like" and how constellations of good (or bad) are drawn to each other to achieve a joint and collective result. It is especially satisfying when a positive or beneficial outlook begins to permeate an opposing mentality or simply extends to a whole society. An example of an "opposing mentality" might be a case where we find ourselves imprisoned in a faction, a fundamentalist group where leisure becomes exploited by destructive stratagems, and dreams by nightmares, devoid of inner balance and peace. One can easily conceive of a terrorist as a highly-motivated, selfless martyr, pure and ecstatic, but if his premise is revenge he has nothing to contribute either to himself or to humanity.

Fortunately, we are moving towards great unifying principles. I believe in a universal religion of simple truths and contemporary relevance. The core of scientific research and its applications has moved from the tangible toward the intangible, from mechanical to electrical, from the power of coal to the power located in the atom. Medically our understanding now encompasses the mind and the brain; we are highly conscious of progress from the body to the mind and now to the living cell, its chemistry and electronics. The general pattern and purpose of life is beginning to emerge as we discover its natural, inevitable occurrence under certain ideal conditions. We realize life's tenacious will to exist and ultimately to experience the revelations of divinity through growing consciousness, communication, and recognition of a process through life and death, through an endless succession and continuity of lives and deaths.

My own essential requirement is to be surrounded by love and trust and I must be able to help and to guide as well as to be helped and guided. The possibilities of learning, helping, of being of use, are infinite. We must respect that holy portion of life which is dreaming, thinking, meditating, conceiving, praying—all uses of leisure time which limit the ego and expand the consciousness. In understanding and caring for another the ego is similarly limited and can return on a higher level. The goal of life is to learn, to give, to be satisfied or content, pleased, to know, to share, and to find satisfaction in the love and grati- tude of another, satisfaction in one's own understanding, in one's own relative health and ability to create or to belong in an environment of reciprocal requirement. Trust, friendship, exuberance, abandon, and joy are essential to civilized existence, as is humor.

Are we capable of taking a new direction along the lines of "intermediate technology" for ourselves and particularly for the "third world," as suggested by E. F. Schumacher in his "small is beautiful" vision? The direction we should take is clear: the means, the understanding, even the willing hands, minds, and hearts are all there. What is missing? We need to discard lethargy and bad habit, scapegoat mentality, prejudice. We need a degree of compulsion, a large portion of inspiration, and a rapid recognition of the profound satisfaction of see- ing happy children, of having trusting friends all over the world, of conquering fears, the persuasive joys of creative living, new learning, and the elation of seeing how much we can achieve for ourselves and by ourselves for others, and for the common good.

Yehudi Menuhin

Books by the Authors

Stanislav Grof

Realms of the Human Unconscious: Observations from LSD Research, Viking Press, New York, 1975; Dutton, New York, 1976

The Human Encounter with Death, Dutton, New York, 1977 (with Joan Halifax)

LSD Psychotherapy, Hunter House, Pomona, CA, 1980

Beyond Death: Gates of Consciousness, Thames & Hudson, London, 1980 (with Christina Grof)

Ancient Wisdom and Modern Science, State University New York (SUNY) Press, Albany, NY, 1984 (ed.)

Beyond the Brain: Birth, Death, and Transcendence in Psychotherapy, SUNY Press, Albany, NY, 1985

The Adventure of Self-Discovery, SUNY Press, Albany, NY, 1987

Human Survival and Consciousness Evolution, SUNY Press, Albany, NY, 1988 (ed.)

Spiritual Emergency: When Personal Transformation Becomes a Crisis, Tarcher, Los Angeles, 1989, (ed. with Christina Grof)

The Stormy Search for the Self: A Guide to Personal Growth Through Transformational Crises, Tarcher, Los Angeles, 1991 (with Christina Grof)

The Holotropic Mind: The Three Levels of Consciousness and How They Shape our Lives, HarperSanFrancisco, CA, (with Hal Zina Bennett), 1994

Books of the Dead: Manuals for Living and Dying, Thames & Hudson, London, 1994

The Cosmic Game: Exploration of the Frontiers of Human Consciousness, SUNY Press, Albany, NY, 1998

Ervin Laszlo

Essential Society: An Ontological Reconstruction, Martinus Nijhoff, The Hague, 1963

Individual, Collectivism, and Political Power, Martinus Nijhoff, The Hague, 1963

Beyond Scepticism and Realism, Martinus Nijhoff, The Hague, 1966

System, Structure, and Experience, Gordon & Breach, New York and London, 1969

La Metaphysique de Whitehead, Martinus Nijhoff, The Hague, 1970

Introduction to Systems Philosophy, Gordon & Breach, New York and London, 1972

The Systems View of the World, George Braziller, New York, 1972; 2nd ed. Hampton Press, Crestkill, NJ, 1996

A Strategy for the Future, George Braziller, New York, 1974

Goals for Mankind: Report to the Club of Rome, Dutton, New York, 1977

The Inner Limits of Mankind, Pergamon Press, Oxford and New York, 1978; 2nd ed., Oneworld Publications, Oxford, 1989

Systems Science and World Order, Pergamon Press, Oxford, 1983

Evolution: The Grand Synthesis, Shambhala New Science, Boston and London, 1987; 2nd ed., Hampton Press, Crestkill, NJ 1996

The Age of Bifurcation, Gordon & Breach, New York and London, 1991

The Creative Cosmos, Floris Books, Edinburgh, 1993

Vision 2020, Gordon & Breach, New York, 1994

The Choice, Putnam/Tarcher, Los Angeles, 1994

The Interconnected Universe, World Scientific, London and Singapore, 1995

The Whispering Pond, Element Books, Shaftesbury and Rockport, 1996; revised ed. 1998

The Insight Edge, Quorum Books, Westport, CA, 1997

Third Millennium: The Challenge and the Vision, Gaia Books, London, 1997

Peter Russell

The TM Technique: A Skeptics Guide, Routledge & Kegan Paul, London and Boston, 1976; Arkana, London, 1990

The Upanishads, Mandala and HarperSanFrancisco, 1990 (ed.)

The Brain Book: Know Your Own Mind and How to Use It, Routledge & Kegan Paul, London; Dutton, New York, 1979

Meditation, BBC Publications, London, 1979

The Awakening Earth, William Morrow, New York, 1993

The Global Brain, Tarcher, Los Angeles, 1983

The Creative Manager: Finding Inner Wisdom in Uncertain Times, Unwin Hyman, London, 1989; Jossey-Bass, San Francisco, 1992

The White Hole in Time: Our Future Evolution and the Meaning of Now, Aquarian, London; HarperSanFrancisco, 1992

The Global Brain Awakens: Our Next Evolutionary Leap, Global Brain, Palo Alto, CA, 1995

Waking Up in Time: Surviving Ever-Accelerating Change, Origin Press, Novato, 1998

Other Readings

Aron, Elaine and Arthur, *The Maharishi Effect: A Revolution through Meditation*, Stillpoint Publishing, Walpole, NH, 1984

Artigiani, Robert, in Ervin Laszlo, Robert Artigiani, Allan Combs, and Vilmos Csányi, *Changing Visions: Human Cognitive Maps Past, Present, and Future*, Adamantine Press, London, 1996

Benor, Daniel J., *Healing Research: Holistic Energy Medicine and Spiritual Healing*, Helix Verlag, Munich, 1993

Bohm, David, *Wholeness and the Implicate Order*, Routledge & Kegan Paul, London, 1980

Capra, Fitzjof and David Steindl-Rast, *Belonging to the Universe*, HarperSanFrancisco, 1983

Davies, P. C. W. and J. R. Brown (eds.). *The Ghost in the Atom*, Cambridge University Press, 1986

Davidson, John, *Subtle Energy*, C. W. Daniel, Saffron Walden, 1983

—— *The Secret of the Creative Vacuum*, C. W. Daniel, Saffron Walden, 1989

Davies, Paul, *God and the New Physics*, Simon & Schuster, New York, 1983

—— *The Mind of God*, Simon & Schuster, New York 1992

—— and John Gribbin, *The Matter Myth*, Simon & Schuster, New York, 1992

Day, William, *Genesis on Planet Earth*, Yale University Press, New Haven, 1984

Dossey, Larry, *Recovering the Soul: A Scientific and Spiritual Search*, Bantam, New York, 1989

—— *Healing Words: The Power of Prayer and the Practice of Medicine*, HarperSanFrancisco, 1993

Eccles John, and Daniel N. Robinson, *The Wonder of Being Human*, Shambhala, London, 1985

Edelman, Gerald M., *Bright Air, Brilliant Fire: On the Matter of Mind*, Basic Books, New York, 1992

Eldredge, Niles, *Unfinished Synthesis. Biological Hierarchies and Modern Evolutionary Thought*, Oxford University Press, 1985
—— *Time Frames: The Rethinking of Darwinian Evolution and the Theory of Punctuated Equilibria*, Simon & Schuster, New York 1985.
Franz, Marie-Louise von, *Psyche and Matter*, Shambhala, Boston and London, 1992,
Gleick, James, *Chaos*, Viking, New York, 1987
Goodwin, Brian, "Development and Evolution," *Journal of Theoretical Biology*, 97, 1982
—— "Organisms and Minds as Organic Forms," *Leonardo*, 22, 1, 1989
Gore, Al, *Earth in the Balance*, Houghton Mifflin, Boston, 1992
Grinberg-Zylverbaum, Jacobo M. Delaflor, M. E. Sanchez-Arellano, M. A. Guevara, and M. Perez, "Human Communication and the Electrophysiological Activity of the Brain," *Subtle Energies*, Vol. 3.3, 1993
Goswami, Amit, *The Self-Aware Universe*, Putnam, New York, 1993
Gray, J., "Consciousness on the Scientific Agenda," *Nature*, 358, 277, 1992
Grosso, Michael, *The Millennium Myth: Love and Death at the End of Time*, Quest, Wheaton, IL, 1995
Hansen, G. M., M. Schlitz and C. Tart, "Summary of Remote Viewing Research," in Russell Targ and K. Harary, *The Mind Race, 1972–1982*, Villard, New York, 1984
Harman, Willis, *Higher Creativity: Liberating the Unconscious for Breakthrough Insight*, Tarcher, Los Angeles, 1984
Harris, Errol E., *Cosmos and Anthropos*, Humanities Press, New York, 1991
Heisenberg, Werner, *Physics and Philosophy*, Harper & Row, New York, 1985
Herbert, Nick, *Elemental Mind*, Dutton, New York, 1993
Hiley, B. J., and David Peat, *Quantum Implications: Essays in Honour of David Bohm*. Routledge and Kegan Paul, London 1987.
Ho, Mae Wan, *The Rainbow and the Worm: The Physics of Organisms*, World Scientific, Singapore and London, 1993
Honorton, C., R. Berger, M. Varvoglis, M. Quant., P. Derr, E. Schechter, and D. Ferrari, "Psi-Communication in the Ganzfeld: Experiments with an Automated Testing System and a Comparison with a Meta-Analysis of Earlier Studies," *Journal of Parapsychology*, 54, 1990
Hoyle, Fred, *The Intelligent Universe*, Michael Joseph, London, 1983
Hoyle, Fred, G. Burbidge and J. V. Narlikar, "A Quasi-Steady State Cosmology Model with Creation of Matter," *The Astrophysical Journal*, 410, 20 June 1993

Huxley, Aldous, *The Perennial Philosophy*, Harper & Row, New York, 1970

Jacob, François, *The Logic of Life: A History of Heredity*, Pantheon, New York, 1970

Jahn R. G., and B. J. Dunne, "On the Quantum Mechanics of Consciousness, with Application to Anomalous Phenomena," *Foundations of Physics*, 16, 8, 1986

Jung, Carl G., "Commentary on *The Secret of the Golden Flower*," in R. Wilhelm, *The Secret of the Golden Flower*, Harcourt, Brace & World, New York, 1962

Kauffman, Stuart, *The Origins of Order: Self-Organization and Selection in Evolution*, Oxford University Press, 1993

Keen, Sam, *Hymns to an Unknown God*, Bantam, New York, 1994

Krippner, S., W. Braud, I. L. Child, J. Palmer, K. R. Rao, M. Schlitz, R. A. White, and J. Utts, "Demonstration Research and Meta-Analysis in Parapsychology," *Journal of Parapsychology*, 57, 1993

Lorimer, David, *Whole In One: The Near-Death Experience and the Ethic of Interconnectedness*, Arkana, London, 1990

Loye, David, (ed.), *The Evolutionary Outrider: The Impact of the Human Agent on Evolution. Essays Honoring Ervin Laszlo*, Fred Praeger, Westport, CN; Adamantine, London, 1998

McKenna, Terence, Rupert Sheldrake and Ralph Abraham, *Trialogues at the Edge of the West*, Bear & Co., Santa Fe, NM, 1992

Morin, Edgar and Anne Brigitte Kern, *Terre-Patrie*, Editions du Seuil, Paris, 1993

Moody, Jr. Raymond A., *The Light Beyond*, Bantam Books, New York, 1988.

—— *Life After Life*, Mockingbird Books, Covington, KY, 1975

Nelson, John E., *Healing the Split*, State University of New York Press, Albany, NY, 1994

Netherton, Morris and Nancy Shiffrin, *Past Lives Therapy*, William Morrow, New York, 1978

Pagels, Heinz, *The Cosmic Code*, Bantam Books, New York, 1990

Peat, F. David, *Einstein's Moon*, Contemporary Books, Chicago, 1990

Penrose, Roger, *The Empereror's New Mind*, Oxford University Press, New York, 1989

Persinger Michael A., and Stanley Krippner, "Dream ESP Experiments and Geomagnetic Activity," *The Journal of the American Society for Psychical Research*, 83, 1989

Polkinghorne, John, *Reason and Reality*, Trinity Press, Philadelphia, 1991

—— *The Quantum World*, Longman, London, 1984

Pribram, Karl, *Brain and Perception: Holonomy and Structure in Figural*

Processing, The MacEachran Lectures, Lawrence Erlbaum, Hillsdale, NJ, 1991

Prigogine, Ilya and Isabelle Stengers, *Order out of Chaos: Man's New Dialogue with Nature*, Bantam Books, New York, 1984

Ray, Paul H., "American Lives," *Noetics Sciences Review*, Spring 1996

Rein, Glen, "Modulation of Neurotransmitter Function by Quantum Fields," *Planetary Association for Clean Energy*, 6, 4, 1993

Requardt, Manfred "From 'Matter-Energy' to 'Irreducible Information Processing'—Arguments for a Paradigm Shift in Fundamental Physics," *Evolution of Information Processing Systems*, K. Haefner (ed.), Springer Verlag, New York and Berlin, 1992

Rosen, Joe, *The Capricious Cosmos*, MacMillan, New York, 1991

Saunders, Peter T., "Evolution without Natural Selection," *Journal of Theoretical Biology*, 1993

Schroeder, Gerald L., *Genesis and the Big Bang*, Bantam Books, New York, 1990

Sheldrake, Rupert., *A New Science of Life*, Blond & Briggs, London, 1981

—— *The Presence of the Past*, Times Books, New York, 1988

Stapp, Henry P., *Matter, Mind, and Quantum Mechanics*, Springer Verlag, New York, 1993

Stevenson, Ian, *Unlearned Language: New Studies in Xenoglossy*, University Press of Virginia, Charlottesville, 1984

—— *Children Who Remember Previous Lives*, University Press of Virginia, Charlottesville, 1987

Stewart, Ian, *Does God Play Dice?*, Blackwell, Cambridge, 1992

Talbot, Michael, *The Holographic Universe*, HarperCollins, New York, 1991

Targ, Russell and K. Harary, *The Mind Race*, Villard Books, New York; 1984.

Tarnas, Richard, *The Passion of the Western Mind*, Ballantine Books, New York, 1993

Tart, Charles, *States of Consciousness*, Dutton, New York, 1975

Tiller, William A., "Subtle Energies in Energy Medicine," *Frontier Perspectives*, 4, 2, Spring 1995

Trefil, James, *Reading the Mind of God*, Anchor Books, New York, 1989

Ullman, M., and S. Krippner, *Dream Studies and Telepathy: An Experimental Approach*, Parapsychology Foundation, New York, 1970

Varvoglis, Mario, "Goal-Directed and Observer-Dependent PK: An Evaluation of the Conformance-Behavior Model and the Observation Theories," *The Journal of the American Society for Psychical Research*, 80, 1986

Weinberg, Steven, *The First Three Minutes*, Basic Books, New York, 1988

—— *Dreams of a Final Theory*, Pantheon Books, New York, 1992

White, John, *The Meeting of Science and Spirit*, Paragon House, New York, 1990

Wigner, Eugene, *The Scientist Speculates*, I. J. Good (ed.), Heinemann, London, 1961

Wilber, Ken, *The Atman Project: A Transpersonal View of Human Development*, Quest Books, Wheaton, 1980

—— *One Taste: The Journals of Ken Wilber, 1997*, Shambhala, Boston, 1999

—— *Quantum Questions*, Shambhala, Boston, 1985, (ed.)

—— *Sex, Ecology, Spirituality; The Spirit of Evolution*, Shambhala, Boston, 1995

Woolger, Roger, *Other Lives, Other Selves*, Doubleday, New York, 1987

Zohar, Danah, *The Quantum Self*, William Morrow, New York, 1990

Zukav, Gary, *The Dancing Wu Li Masters*, Bantam Books, New York, 1989